DATE DUE

JA 29 '93	MY 7 '02	AC 1 '09	
FE 19 '93	MY 28 '02		
	AG 1 '02		
JE '93	NO '03		
JE 22 '93	MY 16 '05		
SE 23 '94	'05		
DE '94	NO 10 '05		
JY 6 '95	AE 1 '05		
NO 3 '95	OE 17 '05		
DE 5 '95	AP 25 '06		
OC 19 '97	AG '06		
'98	OO 30 '06		
NO 3 '98	NO 30 '06		
'00	DE 16 '06		
MY 24 '00	AG '07		
OG 25 '01	FE '07		
	NO '08		

POLICY IMPLICATIONS OF GREENHOUSE WARMING

Policy Implications of Greenhouse Warming—Synthesis Panel

Committee on Science, Engineering, and Public Policy

National Academy of Sciences
National Academy of Engineering
Institute of Medicine

NATIONAL ACADEMY PRESS
Washington, D.C.   1991

ae, N.W. • Washington, D.C. 20418

was approved by the Governing Board
ers are drawn from the councils of the
of Engineering, and the Institute of
is report were chosen for their special
his report is the result of work done by
 committee on Science, Engineering, and Public Policy,
which has authorized its release to the public.

This report has been reviewed by a group other than the authors according to procedures approved by a Report Review Committee and by the Committee on Science, Engineering, and Public Policy. Both consist of members of the National Academy of Sciences, National Academy of Engineering, and Institute of Medicine.

The study reported here was supported by the U.S. Environmental Protection Agency. It also received support from the National Research Council Fund, a pool of private, discretionary, nonfederal funds that is used to support a program of Academy studies of national issues in which science and technology figure significantly. The NRC Fund consists of contributions from a consortium of private foundations including the Carnegie Corporation of New York, the Charles E. Culpeper Foundation, the William and Flora Hewlett Foundation, the John D. and Catherine T. MacArthur Foundation, the Andrew W. Mellon Foundation, the Rockefeller Foundation, and the Alfred P. Sloan Foundation; and the Academy Industry Program, which seeks annual contributions from companies that are concerned with the health of U.S. science and technology and with public policy issues with technological content.

This book is printed on acid-free recycled paper.

Library of Congress Cataloging-in-Publication Data

Committee on Science, Engineering, and Public Policy (U.S.).
    Policy Implications of Greenhouse Warming—Synthesis Panel
        Policy implications of greenhouse warming/
    Policy Implications of Greenhouse Warming—Synthesis Panel, Committee on Science,
    Engineering, and Public Policy, National Academy of Sciences,
    National Academy of Engineering, Institute of Medicine.
        p. cm.
        ISBN 0-309-04440-5 : $14.95
        1. Global warming—Government policy—United States.
    2. Greenhouse effect, Atmospheric—Government policy—United States.
    3. Environmental policy—United States/ I. Title.
    QC981.8.G56C65   1991
    363.73'87—dc20   91-8977
                                                           CIP

Printed in the United States of America
First Printing, April 1991
Second Printing, November 1991

POLICY IMPLICATIONS OF GREENHOUSE WARMING—
SYNTHESIS PANEL

DANIEL J. EVANS (Chairman), Daniel J. Evans & Associates, Seattle, Washington

ROBERT McCORMICK ADAMS, Secretary, Smithsonian Institution, Washington, D.C.

GEORGE F. CARRIER, T. Jefferson Coolidge Professor of Applied Mathematics, Emeritus, Harvard University, Cambridge, Massachusetts

RICHARD N. COOPER, Professor of Economics, Harvard University, Cambridge, Massachusetts

ROBERT A. FROSCH, Vice President, General Motors Research Laboratories, Warren, Michigan

THOMAS H. LEE, Professor Emeritus, Department of Electrical Engineering and Computer Science, Massachusetts Institute of Technology, Cambridge

JESSICA TUCHMAN MATHEWS, Vice President, World Resources Institute, Washington, D.C.

WILLIAM D. NORDHAUS, Professor of Economics, Yale University, New Haven, Connecticut

GORDON H. ORIANS, Professor of Zoology and Director of the Institute for Environmental Studies, University of Washington, Seattle

STEPHEN H. SCHNEIDER, Head, Interdisciplinary Climate Systems, National Center for Atmospheric Research, Boulder, Colorado

MAURICE F. STRONG, Secretary General, United Nations Conference on Environment and Development, New York, New York (resigned from panel February 1990)

SIR CRISPIN TICKELL, Warden, Green College, Oxford, England

VICTORIA J. TSCHINKEL, Senior Consultant, Landers and Parsons, Tallahassee, Florida

PAUL E. WAGGONER, Distinguished Scientist, The Connecticut Agricultural Experiment Station, New Haven

Staff

ROB COPPOCK, Staff Director
DEBORAH D. STINE, Staff Officer
NANCY A. CROWELL, Administrative Specialist
MARION R. ROBERTS, Administrative Secretary

The National Academy of Sciences is a private, nonprofit, self-perpetuating society of distinguished scholars engaged in scientific and engineering research, dedicated to the furtherance of science and technology and to their use for the general welfare. Upon the authority of the charter granted to it by the Congress in 1863, the Academy has a mandate that requires it to advise the federal government on scientific and technical matters. Dr. Frank Press is president of the National Academy of Sciences.

The National Academy of Engineering was established in 1964, under the charter of the National Academy of Sciences, as a parallel organization of outstanding engineers. It is autonomous in its administration and in the selection of its members, sharing with the National Academy of Sciences the responsibility for advising the federal government. The National Academy of Engineering also sponsors engineering programs aimed at meeting national needs, encourages education and research, and recognizes the superior achievements of engineers. Dr. Robert M. White is president of the National Academy of Engineering.

The Institute of Medicine was established in 1970 by the National Academy of Sciences to secure the services of eminent members of appropriate professions in the examination of policy matters pertaining to the health of the public. The Institute acts under the responsibility given to the National Academy of Sciences by its congressional charter to be an adviser to the federal government and, upon its own initiative, to identify issues of medical care, research, and education. Dr. Samuel O. Thier is president of the Institute of Medicine.

The Committee on Science, Engineering, and Public Policy (COSEPUP) is a joint committee of the National Academy of Sciences, the National Academy of Engineering, and the Institute of Medicine. It includes members of the councils of all three bodies.

Preface

Greenhouse gases and global warming have received increasing attention in recent years. The identification of the antarctic ozone hole in 1985 combined with the hot, dry summer of 1988 to provide the drama that seems to be required for capturing national media coverage. Emerging scientific results, including findings about greenhouse gases other than carbon dioxide, added to the interest.

One consequence was congressional action. The HUD–Independent Agencies Appropriations Act of 1988 (House Report 100-701:26) called for

> a NAS study on global climate change. This study should establish the scientific consensus on the rate and magnitude of climate change, estimate the projected impacts, and evaluate policy options for mitigating and responding to such changes. The need for and utility of improved temperature monitoring capabilities should also be examined, as resources permit.

According to subsequent advice received from members of Congress, the study was to focus on radiatively active trace gases from human sources, or "greenhouse warming." This report is one of the products of that study.

The study was conducted under the auspices of the Committee on Science, Engineering, and Public Policy, a unit of the councils of the National Academy of Sciences, the National Academy of Engineering, and the Institute of Medicine. The study involved nearly 50 experts, including scientists as well as individuals with experience in government, private industry, and public interest organizations.

The study was conducted by four panels that did their work in parallel, but with considerable exchange of information and some overlap in membership. The Synthesis Panel (whose membership is listed on page iii) was charged with developing overall findings and recommendations. The Effects Panel examined what is known about changing climatic conditions and related effects. The Mitigation Panel looked at options for reducing or reversing the onset of potential global warming. The Adaptation Panel assessed the impacts of possible climate change on human and ecologic systems and the policies that could help people and natural systems adapt to those changes. The members of these panels are listed in Appendix C.

This is the report of the Synthesis Panel. The reports of all four panels will be published by the National Academy Press in a single volume.

The panels conducted their analyses simultaneously between September 1989 and January 1991. The chairmen of the Effects, Mitigation, and Adaptation panels were members of the Synthesis Panel. Several members of the Synthesis Panel also were members of other panels. In its deliberations, however, the Synthesis Panel considered more than just the reports of the other panels. It also heard from experts with a range of views on the policy relevance of computer simulation models, widely held to be the best available tools for projecting climate change, and of economic models used to assess consequences of policies to reduce greenhouse gas emissions. The study also drew upon the report of the Intergovernmental Panel on Climate Change, an international effort released during the course of the study. Several members of the various study panels also contributed to that effort. Finally, the study drew upon other Academy studies. For example, in its examination of sea level change, the panel used analyses from the following reports: *Glaciers, Ice Sheets, and Sea Level: Effects of a CO_2-Induced Climatic Change* (National Academy Press, 1985), *Responding to Changes in Sea Level: Engineering Implications* (National Academy Press, 1987), and *Sea Level Change* (National Academy Press, 1990). The report of the Synthesis Panel is thus more than a summary of the assessments performed by the other three panels. It contains topics beyond those covered by the other panels and reflects the deliberations and judgments of the Synthesis Panel.

The report identifies what should be done now to counter potential greenhouse warming or deal with its likely consequences. The recommendations of the Synthesis Panel, if followed, should provide the United States with a framework for responding to this very important concern.

> The Honorable Daniel J. Evans, Chairman
> Policy Implications of Greenhouse Warming—Synthesis Panel

Acknowledgments

The work of the other panels was indispensable in the preparation of this report. George F. Carrier was chairman of the Effects Panel; Thomas H. Lee was chairman of the Mitigation Panel; and Paul E. Waggoner was chairman of the Adaptation Panel. Full membership lists for the other panels are given in Appendix C.

While this report represents the work of the Synthesis Panel, it would not have been produced without the support of professional staff from the Committee on Science, Engineering, and Public Policy of the National Academy of Sciences, National Academy of Engineering, and Institute of Medicine: Rob Coppock, who drafted the chapters and the question and answers section (Appendix A), and refined them on the basis of the panel's discussions and conclusions, and Deborah Stine, whose work on the Mitigation Panel report is reflected in Chapter 6. Nancy Crowell contributed to preparation of the Adaptation and Mitigation panel reports and the administrative organization of the study. Their resumes are included with those of the panel in Appendix B because of their intellectual contributions, which advanced the committee's efforts throughout the study. The report was greatly improved by the diligent work of its editor, Roseanne Price. In addition, invaluable support was provided by Marion Roberts.

The panel also acknowledges with appreciation presentations made at meetings of the Synthesis Panel by the following persons:

Frederick Bernthal, Assistant Secretary of State
Roger Dower, World Resources Institute
Jae Edmonds, Battelle Northwest Laboratories
James Hansen, Goddard Institute for Space Studies
Dale Jorgenson, Harvard University

Richard Lindzen, Massachusetts Institute of Technology
Gordon MacDonald, MITRE Corporation
Alan Manne, Stanford University
Richard Morgenstern, U.S. Environmental Protection Agency
Veerabhadran Ramanathan, University of Chicago
William Reifsnyder, Yale University
Kevin Trenberth, National Center for Atmospheric Research
Robert Williams, Princeton University
Timothy E. Wirth, United States Senator

Contents

1 INTRODUCTION 1

2 BACKGROUND 3
   The Global Nature of Greenhouse Warming, 3
   Greenhouse Gas Emissions from Human Activities, 3
   The Effects of World Population and Economic Growth, 4
   Trends in Human Activities Affecting Greenhouse Gas
      Concentrations, 5

3 THE GREENHOUSE GASES AND THEIR EFFECTS 10
   Earth's Radiation Balance, 12
   What We Can Learn from Climate Models, 17
   What We Can Learn from the Temperature Record, 20
   Sea Level, 23
   Possible Dramatic Changes, 24
   Conclusions, 24

4 POLICY FRAMEWORK 27
   Comparing Mitigation and Adaptation, 27
   Assigning Values to Future Outcomes, 29
   A Method for Comparing Options, 30
      Assessing Mitigation Options, 31
      Assessing Adaptation Options, 32
   Other Factors Affecting Policy Choices About
      Greenhouse Warming, 33

5 ADAPTATION 34
    Methods of Adaptation, 34
    The Role of Innovation, 35
    Assessing Impacts and Adaptive Capacity, 36
        CO_2 Fertilization of Green Plants, 36
        Agriculture, 37
        Managed Forests and Grasslands, 37
        Natural Landscape, 37
        Marine and Coastal Environments, 38
        Water Resources, 38
        Industry and Energy, 39
        Tourism and Recreation, 39
        Settlements and Coastal Structures, 39
        Human Health, 39
        Migration, 40
        Political Tranquility, 40
    Some Important Indices, 40
    Evaluating Adaptation Options, 41
    Adapting to Climate Change, 42
        Activities with Low Sensitivity, 42
        Activities That Are Sensitive But Can Be Adapted at a Cost, 42
        Activities That Are Sensitive with Questionable Adjustment
            or Adaptation, 44
        Cataclysmic Climatic Changes, 44
    Conclusions, 45

6 MITIGATION 47
    The Role of Cost-Effectiveness, 48
    Technological Costing Versus Energy Modeling, 48
    Planning a Cost-Effective Policy, 49
    An Assessment of Mitigation Options in the United States, 51
    Comparing Options, 60
    Implementing Mitigation Options, 62
    Conclusions, 63

7 INTERNATIONAL CONSIDERATIONS 64
    International Activities, 65
    Future International Agreements, 66
    Other Actions, 66

8 FINDINGS AND CONCLUSIONS 67
    Policy Considerations, 68
        Capacities of Industrialized and Developing Countries, 68

Taxes and Incentives, 69
Fundamental and Applied Research, 69
A Proposed Framework for Responding to the Threat of
    Greenhouse Warming, 70
General Conclusions, 71

9 RECOMMENDATIONS 72
Reducing or Offsetting Emissions of Greenhouse Gases, 72
    Halocarbon Emissions, 73
    Energy Policy, 73
    Forest Offsets, 75
Enhancing Adaptation to Greenhouse Warming, 76
Improving Knowledge for Future Decisions, 78
Evaluating Geoengineering Options, 80
Exercising International Leadership, 81

APPENDIXES

A QUESTIONS AND ANSWERS ABOUT GREENHOUSE
    WARMING 85
The Greenhouse Effect: What Is Known, What Can Be Predicted, 85
A Framework for Responding to Additional Greenhouse Warming, 96
Impacts of Additional Greenhouse Warming, 97
Preventing or Reducing Additional Greenhouse Warming, 103
Adapting to Additional Greenhouse Warming, 107
Implementing Response Programs, 109
Actions to be Taken, 110

B BACKGROUND INFORMATION ON SYNTHESIS PANEL
    MEMBERS AND PROFESSIONAL STAFF 114

C MEMBERSHIP LISTS FOR EFFECTS, MITIGATION, AND
    ADAPTATION PANELS................................... 117

INDEX 121

POLICY IMPLICATIONS OF GREENHOUSE WARMING

1

Introduction

Greenhouse gases in the atmosphere have an important influence on the climate of our planet. Simply stated, greenhouse gases impede the outward flow of infrared radiation more effectively than they impede incoming solar radiation. Because of this asymmetry, the earth, its atmosphere, and its oceans are warmer than they would be in the absence of such gases.

The major greenhouse gases are water vapor, carbon dioxide (CO_2), methane (CH_4), chlorofluorocarbons (CFCs) and hydrogenated chlorofluorocarbons (HCFCs), ozone (O_3), and nitrous oxide (N_2O). Without the naturally occurring greenhouse gases (principally water vapor and CO_2), the earth's average temperature would be about 33°C (59°F) colder than it is, and the planet would be much less suitable for human habitation.

Human activity has contributed to increased atmospheric concentrations of CO_2, CH_4, and CFCs. The increased atmospheric concentrations of greenhouse gases may increase average global temperatures. The possible warming due to increased concentrations of these gases is called "greenhouse warming." The atmospheric concentration of CO_2 in 1990 was 353 parts per million by volume (ppmv), about 25 percent greater than it was before the Industrial Revolution (about 280 ± 10 ppmv prior to 1750). Atmospheric CO_2 is increasing at about 0.5 percent per year. The concentration of CH_4 was 1.72 ppmv in 1990, or slightly more than twice that before 1750. It is rising at a rate of 0.9 percent per year. CFCs do not occur naturally and were not found in the atmosphere until production began a few decades ago. Continued increases in atmospheric concentrations of greenhouse gases would affect the earth's radiative balance and might cause a significant amount of additional greenhouse warming.

General circulation models (GCMs) are the principal tools used to project climatic changes. At their present level of development, GCMs project that an increase in greenhouse gas concentrations equivalent to a doubling of the preindustrial level of atmospheric CO_2 would produce global average temperature increases between 1.9° and 5.2°C (3.4° and 9.4°F). The larger of these temperature increases would mean a climate warmer than any in human history. The consequences of this amount of warming are unknown and could include extremely unpleasant surprises.

During the last 100 years the average global temperature has increased between 0.3° and 0.6°C (0.5° and 1.1°F). This temperature rise could be attributable to greenhouse warming or to natural climate variability; with today's limited understanding of the underlying phenomena, neither can be ruled out.

Increases in atmospheric greenhouse gas concentrations probably will be followed by increases in average atmospheric temperature. We cannot predict how rapidly these changes will occur, how intense they will be for any given atmospheric concentration, or, in particular, what regional changes in temperature, precipitation, wind speed, and frost occurrence can be expected. So far, no large or rapid increases in the global average temperature have occurred, and there is no evidence yet of imminent rapid change. But if the higher GCM projections prove to be accurate, substantial responses would be needed, and the stresses on this planet and its inhabitants would be serious.

It is against this backdrop that prudent, necessarily international, plans should be made and actions undertaken. These plans and actions should start with responses justified by the current credibility of the threat. They also should include preparatory measures that can set the stage for more far reaching responses if the evidence of need becomes persuasive. It is in this setting that the panel performed its analyses and developed recommendations for action by the United States.

The principal findings and conclusions of the panel are summarized in Chapter 8, and its recommendations are in Chapter 9. Following the report is an appendix called "Questions and Answers About Greenhouse Warming," which discusses relevant issues in a format the panel believes may be especially useful to the reader.

2

Background

THE GLOBAL NATURE OF GREENHOUSE WARMING

Greenhouse warming is global in at least two respects. First, greenhouse gases released anywhere in the world disperse rapidly in the global atmosphere. Neither the location of release nor the activity resulting in a release makes much difference. A molecule of CO_2 from a cooking fire in Yellowstone or India is subject to the same laws of chemistry and physics in the atmosphere as a molecule from the exhaust pipe of a high-performance auto in Indiana or Europe. Second, the anticipated climatic effects include changes in the global circulation of air and water. Global average temperature is often used as an indicator of the various climatic effects. Climate change, however, has many facets: seasonal cycles and annual fluctuations of temperature and precipitation, wind speed and direction, and strength and direction of ocean currents. Although the results of climate change will differ from place to place, they derive from global processes.

GREENHOUSE GAS EMISSIONS FROM HUMAN ACTIVITIES

Greenhouse warming is complicated in another, more fundamental way. The amounts released vary, of course, but virtually every form of human activity contributes some amount of greenhouse gas to the atmosphere or removes some from the atmosphere. Subsistence agriculture contributes its bit, as does modern industry and the consumption and use of modern goods and services. Growing trees remove CO_2 from the atmosphere, but burning wood for heating and cooking releases CO_2 into the atmosphere. Rice paddies and cattle contribute CH_4. Industrial activities include releases of all the

greenhouse gases to varying extents. In most societies the burning of fossil
fuels for electricity and transportation is a major contributor.

Since releases of greenhouse gases are connected to most economic activity, significant reductions in their emission may affect the economic
competitiveness of individuals, firms, and nations. Avoiding additional
greenhouse warming may be costly, it may create economic winners and
losers, and it may alter trade balances.

THE EFFECTS OF WORLD POPULATION AND ECONOMIC GROWTH

The world's population today is 5.3 billion, and it is expected to continue
to grow at about 1.7 percent per year at current rates of fertility. Figure 2.1
shows historical population growth and an estimate for 2000. This increasing
population is one of the major factors affecting trends in greenhouse gas
emissions. More people create greater demand for food, energy, clothing,
and shelter. Producing such products emits greenhouse gases.

Economic growth also produces more greenhouse gas emissions. If population
grows with constant per capita income, more resources are used for food,
clothing, and shelter. If per capita income grows in a constant population,
the demand for goods also grows, particularly for health and education
services, transportation, and housing. Most nations in the world have policies to reduce population growth rates, but all nations seek to achieve rapid
growth in per capita income. The reduction of greenhouse gas emissions is
well served by the first objective (reducing population growth) but, depending on the means used, can be in conflict with the second (growth in per
capita income).

The detailed links between population growth and greenhouse gas emissions are complex and not well understood. The developing countries that
have reduced their population growth rates within the last 30 years did so
only after rapidly increasing their standards of living. This often was accompanied
by environmental degradation. Perhaps it will be possible to rapidly raise
living standards without resulting in traditional patterns of pollution. Unfortunately, there are few examples to guide us. What is needed is a breakthrough
in strategies for development, especially with respect to energy supply and
demand.   Developing countries experiencing rapid economic growth will
need effective mitigation programs if they are to avoid substantial increases
in their greenhouse gas emissions. Implementing new strategies will require
funds that will probably be scarce if populations grow rapidly. Nevertheless, at any given per capita rate of greenhouse gas emissions, a smaller
population means fewer emissions, as well as less stress on the environment
in general.

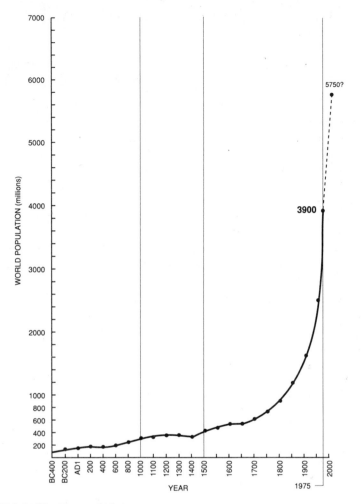

FIGURE 2.1 World population.

SOURCE: C. McEvedy and R. Jones. 1978. *Atlas of World Population History.*
Middlesex, United Kingdom: Penguin. Figure 6.2.

TRENDS IN HUMAN ACTIVITIES AFFECTING
GREENHOUSE GAS CONCENTRATIONS

Table 2.1 presents emission estimates for five greenhouse gases (CO_2, CH_4, CFC-11, CFC-12, and N_2O) that accounted for about 87 percent of the increase in the heat-trapping capacity of the atmosphere in the 1980s and about 92 percent of the increase over the previous 100 years. The table presents estimated 1985 emissions (in million tons per year) and converts non-CO_2

TABLE 2.1 Estimated 1985 Global Greenhouse Gas Emissions from Human Activities

	Greenhouse Gas Emissions (Mt/yr)	CO_2-equivalent Emissions[a] (Mt/yr)	
CO_2 Emissions			
Commercial energy	18,800	18,800	(57)
Tropical deforestation	2,600	2,600	(8)
Other	400	400	(1)
TOTAL	21,800	21,800	(66)
CH_4 Emissions			
Fuel production	60	1,300	(4)
Enteric fermentation	70	1,500	(5)
Rice cultivation	110	2,300	(7)
Landfills	30	600	(2)
Tropical deforestation	20	400	(1)
Other	30	600	(2)
TOTAL	320	6,700	(20)[b]
CFC-11 and CFC-12 Emissions			
TOTAL	0.6	3,200	(10)
N_2O Emissions			
Coal combustion	1	290	(>1)
Fertilizer use	1.5	440	(1)
Gain of cultivated land	0.4	120	(>1)
Tropical deforestation	0.5	150	(>1)
Fuel wood and industrial biomass	0.2	60	(>1)
Agricultural wastes	0.4	120	(>1)
TOTAL	4	1,180	(4)
TOTAL		32,880	(100)

[a]CO_2-equivalent emissions are calculated from the Greenhouse Gas Emissions column by using the following multipliers:

CO_2	1
CH_4	21
CFC-11 and -12	5,400
N_2O	290

Numbers in parentheses are percentages of total.

[b]Total does not sum due to rounding errors.

NOTE: Mt/yr = million (10^6) metric tons (t) per year. All entries are rounded because the exact values are controversial.

SOURCE: Adapted from U.S. Department of Energy. 1990. *The Economics of Long-Term Global Climate Change: A Preliminary Assessment—Report of an Interagency Task Force.* Springfield, Va.: National Technical Information Service.

TABLE 2.2 Carbon Dioxide Emission Estimates

	1960		1970		1980		1988	
	Total	Per Capita	Total	Per Capita	Total	Per Capita	Total	Per Capita
East Germany	263.6	15.4	160.6	15.8	306.9	18.3	327.4	19.8
United States	2858.2	16.1	4273.5	20.9	4617.4	20.2	4804.1	19.4
Canada	193.2	10.6	333.3	15.4	424.6	17.6	437.8	16.9
Czechoslovakia	129.8	9.5	199.1	13.9	242.4	15.8	233.6	15.0
Australia	88.4	8.4	142.6	11.4	202.8	13.9	241.3	14.7
USSR	1452.4	6.6	2303.4	9.5	3283.5	12.5	3982.0	13.9
Poland	201.7	7.0	303.6	9.2	459.8	12.8	459.4	12.1
West Germany	544.9	9.9	736.6	12.1	762.7	12.5	669.9	11.0
United Kingdom	589.6	11.4	643.1	11.4	588.9	10.3	559.2	9.9
Romania	53.5	2.9	119.5	5.9	199.8	9.2	220.7	9.5
South Africa	98.6	5.5	149.6	6.6	213.4	7.7	284.2	8.4
Japan	234.3	2.6	742.1	7.3	934.6	8.1	989.3	8.1
Italy	110.4	2.2	286.0	5.5	372.5	6.6	359.7	6.2
France	274.3	5.9	426.1	8.4	484.4	9.2	320.1	5.9
Korea	49.1	0.4	52.1	1.5	125.8	3.3	204.6	4.8
Spain	12.8	1.5	110.7	3.3	198.7	5.5	187.7	4.8
Mexico	63.1	1.8	106.0	1.8	260.3	3.7	306.9	3.7
People's Republic of China	789.4	1.2	775.9	1.0	1490.1	1.5	2236.3	2.1
Brazil	46.9	0.7	86.5	0.7	176.7	1.5	202.4	1.5
India	121.7	0.4	195.4	0.4	350.2	0.4	600.6	0.7

NOTE: Emission estimates are rounded and expressed in million tons of CO_2; per capita estimates are rounded and expressed in tons of CO_2. All tons are metric.

SOURCE: Adapted from Thomas A. Boden, Paul Kanciruk, and Michael P. Farrell. 1990. *Trends '90: A Compendium of Data on Global Change.* Oak Ridge, Tenn.: Oak Ridge National Laboratory.

gases into CO_2-equivalent emissions so that their respective contributions can be compared. These projections necessarily involve uncertainties. (Note that throughout this report tons (t) are metric; 1 Mt equals 1 million metric tons.)

The United States is the world's largest contributor of greenhouse gas emissions. Table 2.2 shows total and per capita CO_2 emissions (the dominant greenhouse gas emitted by human activity) for the United States and several other countries from 1960 to 1988, in order of their most recent per capita emissions. Two of the six countries with the largest total emissions are developing countries (People's Republic of China and India). Per capita

TABLE 2.3 Carbon Dioxide Emissions per Unit of Economic Activity (1988 to 1989)

	Emissions (Mt CO_2/yr)	GNP (billions of $/yr)	Emissions/GNP Ratio (Mt CO_2/$1000 GNP)
China	2236.3	372.3[a]	6.01[b]
South Africa	284.2	79.0	3.60
Romania	220.7	79.8[a]	2.77[b]
Poland	459.4	172.4[a]	2.66[b]
India	600.6	237.9	2.52
East Germany	327.4	159.5[a]	2.05[b]
Czechoslovakia	233.6	123.2[a]	1.90[b]
Mexico	306.9	176.7	1.74
USSR	3982.0	2659.5[a]	1.50[b]
South Korea	204.6	171.3	1.19
Canada	437.8	435.9	1.00
United States	4804.1	4880.1	0.98
Australia	241.3	246.0	0.98
United Kingdom	559.2	702.4	0.80
Brazil	202.4	323.6	0.63
West Germany	669.9	1201.8	0.56
Spain	187.7	340.3	0.55
Italy	359.7	828.9	0.43
Japan	989.3	2843.7	0.35
France	320.1	949.4	0.34

[a]Estimates of GNP for centrally planned economies are subject to large margins of error. These estimates are as much as 100 times larger than those from other sources that correct for availability of goods or use free-market exchange rates.

[b]The emissions/GNP is also likely to be underestimated for centrally planned economies.

SOURCE: Table 2.2 above for CO_2 emissions. For GNP, entries are from World Bank, 1990, *World Development Report, 1990,* World Bank, Washington, D.C., Table 3. For centrally planned economies other than China, estimates are from U.S. Central Intelligence Agency, *World Factbook 1990.*

emissions in 1988 are lower than those in 1980 in several countries, including the United States, suggesting that some actions to reduce greenhouse warming are already being taken.

It is also informative to compare emissions to economic activity. Table 2.3 shows CO_2 emissions per unit of economic activity for recent emissions data. The table illustrates that some developing countries and centrally planned economies are large emitters of greenhouse gases per unit of

TABLE 2.4 Estimated Deforestation in the Tropics (thousand hectares)

	Number of Countries Studied	Total Land Area	Forest Area 1980	Forest Area 1990	Annual Deforestation 1980-1990
Africa	15	609,500	289,700	241,500	4,800
Latin America	32	1,263,500	825,900	753,000	7,300
Asia	15	891,100	334,500	287,500	4,700
TOTAL	62	2,754,500	1,450,100	1,282,300	15,800

NOTE: Entries cover closed tropical forests. Closed forests have trees covering a high proportion of the ground and grass does not form a continuous layer on the forest floor. The numbers are indicative and should not be taken as regional averages.

SOURCE: Committee on Forestry. 1990. *Interim Report on Forest Resources Assessment 1990 Project,* Tenth Session. Geneva, Switzerland: Food and Agricultural Organization of the United Nations.

economic activity and that the United States is in the middle of the field. It also shows France with low emissions per unit of economic activity, probably because of its extensive reliance on nuclear power as a source of electricity.

Table 2.4 shows recent estimates of deforestation in tropical forests for selected countries. About 80 percent of this wood is destroyed or used as fuel wood, and the remaining 20 percent is harvested for industrial or trade purposes. If the trees are burned, the CO_2 they have stored is added to the air, and if they are replaced with plants that grow more slowly, less CO_2 will be removed from the atmosphere.

3

The Greenhouse Gases and Their Effects

Atmospheric concentrations of greenhouse gases are increasingly well known. Current concentrations, emission accumulation rates, and atmospheric lifetimes of key gases are summarized in Table 3.1. Past releases of these gases are less well documented. As shown in Figure 3.1, atmospheric CO_2 began increasing in the eighteenth century. Regular monitoring, begun in 1958, shows an accelerated increase in atmospheric CO_2. About a decade of data also documents rapidly increasing atmospheric concentrations of CH_4. Indirect evidence from tree rings, air bubbles trapped in glacial ice as it formed, and other sources has been used to reconstruct past concentrations of these gases.

The dispersion and transformation of greenhouse gases in the atmosphere are also fairly well understood. There is, however, one important exception: CO_2. Recent measurements indicate that about 40 percent of the CO_2 released into the atmosphere stays there for decades at least, and about 15 percent seems to be incorporated into the upper layers of the oceans. The location of the remaining 45 percent of the CO_2 from human activity is not known. Until the redistribution of newly emitted CO_2 is more thoroughly understood, reliable projections of the rate of increase of atmospheric CO_2 will lack credibility even for precisely estimated emission rates. Even so, it is probably sensible during the next decade or two to use 40 percent of CO_2 emissions as an estimate of the atmospheric accumulation rate. On a longer time scale, there is, as of now, no estimation procedure that merits confidence.

Each greenhouse gas is subject to different chemical reactions in the atmosphere and to different mechanisms of alteration or removal. Thus projections of future concentrations must account not only for emissions but also for transformations in the atmosphere. In addition, the various greenhouse gases have different energy-absorbing properties. For example, each molecule

TABLE 3.1 Key Greenhouse Gases Influenced by Human Activity

	CO_2	CH_4	CFC-11	CFC-12	N_2O
Preindustrial atmospheric concentration	280 ppmv	0.8 ppmv	0	0	288 ppbv
Current atmospheric concentration (1990)[a]	353 ppmv	1.72 ppmv	280 pptv	484 pptv	310 ppbv
Current rate of annual atmospheric accumulation[b]	1.8 ppmv (0.5%)	0.015 ppmv (0.9%)	9.5 pptv (4%)	17 pptv (4%)	0.8 ppbv (0.25%)
Atmospheric lifetime (years)[c]	(50-200)	10	65	130	150

[a]The 1990 concentrations have been estimated on the basis of an extrapolation of measurements reported for earlier years, assuming that the recent trends remained approximately constant.

[b]Net annual emissions of CO_2 from the biosphere not affected by human activity, such as volcanic emissions, are assumed to be small. Estimates of human-induced emissions from the biosphere are controversial.

[c]For each gas in the table, except CO_2, the "lifetime" is defined as the ratio of the atmospheric concentration to the total rate of removal. This time scale also characterizes the rate of adjustment of the atmospheric concentrations if the emission rates are changed abruptly. CO_2 is a special case because it is merely circulated among various reservoirs (atmosphere, ocean, biota). The "lifetime" of CO_2 given in the table is a rough indication of the time it would take for the CO_2 concentration to adjust to changes in the emissions.

NOTES: Ozone has not been included in the table because of lack of precise data. Here ppmv = parts per million by volume, ppbv = parts per billion by volume, and pptv = parts per trillion by volume.

SOURCE: World Meteorological Organization. 1990. *Climate Change, the IPCC Scientific Assessment*. Cambridge, United Kingdom: Cambridge University Press. Table 1.1. Reprinted by permission of Cambridge University Press.

of CH_4 absorbs radiative energy 25 times more effectively than each molecule of CO_2, and CFC-12 is 15,800 times more effective than CO_2 on a per molecule basis and, since molecules of the two gases have different mass, 5,750 times more effective on a per mass basis. Figure 3.2 incorporates a simple extrapolation of current atmospheric transformation rates. It displays the incremental energy absorption rates that would accompany various emission scenarios. The energy absorption is given in watts per square meter (W/m^2) and, in accord with the vocabulary of this subject, changes in the absorption are called "radiative forcing." The curves show the aggregate contribution of each gas for the period from 1990 to 2030.

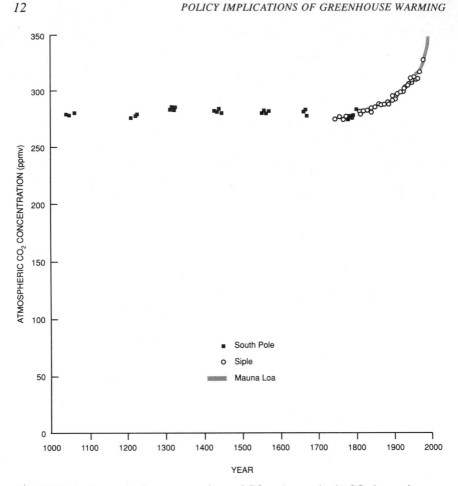

FIGURE 3.1 Atmospheric concentrations of CO_2. Atmospheric CO_2 began increasing in the eighteenth century. Direct measurements made at the Mauna Loa Observatory in Hawaii since 1958 indicate that the increase has accelerated.

SOURCE: Adapted from W. M. Post, T.-H. Peng, W. R. Emanuel, A. W. King, V. H. Dale, and D. DeAngelis. 1990. The global carbon cycle. *American Scientist* 78(4):310-326, Figure 3b.

EARTH'S RADIATION BALANCE

The climatic system of the earth is driven by radiant energy from the sun. Incoming solar radiation at the top of the earth's atmosphere has an average intensity, over the year and over the globe, of 340 W/m². Over the long time periods during which the climate is steady, the radiation from the top of the atmosphere to space has, again on average, the same intensity. As can be seen in Figure 3.3, the incoming arrows, representing the incoming intensity

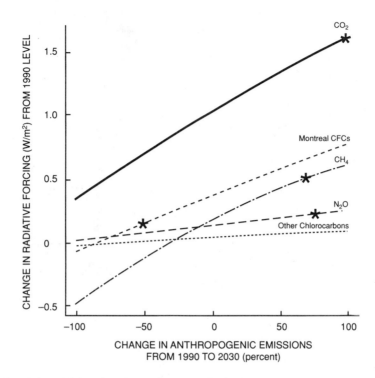

FIGURE 3.2 Additional radiative forcing of principal greenhouse gases from 1990
to 2030 for different emission rates. The horizontal axis shows changes in greenhouse gas emissions ranging from completely eliminating emissions (−100 percent)
to doubling current emissions (+100 percent). Emission changes are assumed to be
linear from 1990 levels to the 2030 level selected. The vertical axis shows the
change in radiative forcing in watts per square meter at the earth's surface in 2030.
Each asterisk indicates the projected emissions of that gas assuming no additional
regulatory policies, based on the Intergovernmental Panel on Climate Change estimates
and the original restrictions agreed to under the Montreal Protocol, which limits
emissions of CFCs. Chemical interactions among greenhouse gas species are not
included.

For CO_2 emissions remaining at 1990 levels through 2030, the resulting change
in radiative forcing can be determined in two steps: (1) Find the point on the curve
labeled "CO_2" that is vertically above 0 percent change on the bottom scale. (2) The
radiative forcing on the surface-troposphere system can be read in watts per square
meter by moving horizontally to the left-hand scale, or about 1 W/m². These steps
must be repeated for each gas. For example, the radiative forcing for continued
1990-level emissions of CH_4 through 2030 would be about 0.2 W/m².

SOURCE: Chapter 3 of the report of the Effects Panel.

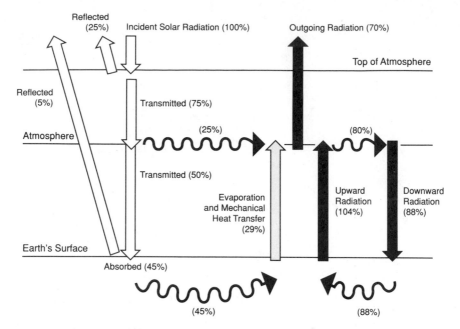

FIGURE 3.3 Earth's radiation balance. The solar radiation is set at 100 percent; all other values are in relation to it. About 25 percent of incident solar radiation is reflected back into space by the atmosphere, about 25 percent is absorbed by gases in the atmosphere, and about 5 percent is reflected into space from the earth's surface, leaving 45 percent to be absorbed by the oceans, land, and biotic material (white arrows).

Evaporation and mechanical heat transfer inject energy into the atmosphere equal to about 29 percent of incident radiation (grey arrow). Radiative energy emissions from the earth's surface and from the atmosphere (straight black arrows) are determined by the temperatures of the earth's surface and the atmosphere, respectively. Upward energy radiation from the earth's surface is about 104 percent of incident solar radiation. Atmospheric gases absorb part (25 percent) of the solar radiation penetrating the top of the atmosphere and all of the mechanical heat transferred from the earth's surface and the outbound radiation from the earth's surface. The downward radiation from the atmosphere is about 88 percent and outgoing radiation about 70 percent of incident solar radiation.

Note that the amounts of outgoing and incoming radiation balance at the top of the atmosphere, at 100 percent of incoming solar radiation (which is balanced by 5 percent reflected from the surface, 25 percent reflected from the top of the atmosphere, and 70 percent outgoing radiation), and at the earth's surface, at 133 percent (45 percent absorbed solar radiation plus 88 percent downward radiation from the atmosphere balanced by 29 percent evaporation and mechanical heat transfer and 104 percent upward radiation). Energy transfers into and away from the atmosphere also balance, at the atmosphere line, at 208 percent of incident solar radiation (75 percent transmitted solar radiation plus 29 percent mechanical transfer from the

or energy flux, balance the outgoing arrows at the top of the atmosphere. The figure shows a similar balance at the earth's surface. The downward flow of energy at the earth's surface is 133 percent of the incident solar radiation (the 45 percent of the incident solar radiation absorbed from the incoming energy flow plus the 88 percent downward infrared radiation). The combined downward transfer of energy at the earth's surface is greater than that arriving at the top of the atmosphere because the atmosphere, since it has a temperature greater than absolute zero, also emits energy. The energy emitted by the atmosphere adds to that arriving at the surface. The energy arriving at the earth's surface is balanced by that leaving the surface (the 29 percent evaporation and mechanical heat transfer and the 104 percent upward infrared radiation). Similarly, the flow of energy into the atmosphere (incoming solar radiation not reflected from the top of the atmosphere, outbound evaporation and mechanical heat transfer, and upward infrared radiation from the earth's surface) balances the flow of energy away from the atmosphere (incoming solar radiation transmitted to the earth's surface, outgoing infrared radiation, and downward infrared radiation).

Some of the numbers shown in Figure 3.3 depend on the state of the atmosphere, for example, its temperature, greenhouse gas content, cloud distribution, and wind distribution. Others depend on the temperature of the land and ocean surfaces and/or on the ice cover. Changes in any and all of these characterizing features can produce changes in the individual heat fluxes and, in particular, changes in atmospheric and/or oceanic temperature. These can lead to changes in cloud cover and humidity that, in turn, induce further changes in the state of the atmosphere. In addition, both the interdependencies of the individual heat transfer contributions illustrated in Figure 3.2 and the (partial) list of possible changes in characterizing features just mentioned imply that increases in greenhouse gas concentrations will lead to modifications of the climate.

It is important to recognize that these climate modifications are not instantaneous responses to the gas concentration changes that produce them. There is always a transient period, or "lag," before the equilibrium tempera-

---

surface plus 104 percent upward radiation balanced by 50 percent of incoming solar continuing to the earth's surface, 70 percent outgoing radiation, and 88 percent downward radiation). These different energy transfers are due to the heat-trapping effects of the greenhouse gases in the atmosphere, the reemission of energy absorbed by these gases, and the cycling of energy through the various components in the diagram. The accuracy of the numbers in the diagram is typically ±5.

This diagram pertains to a period during which the climate is steady (or unchanging); that is, there is no net change in heat transfers into earth's surface, no net change in heat transfers into the atmosphere, and no net radiation change into the atmosphere-earth system from beyond the atmosphere.

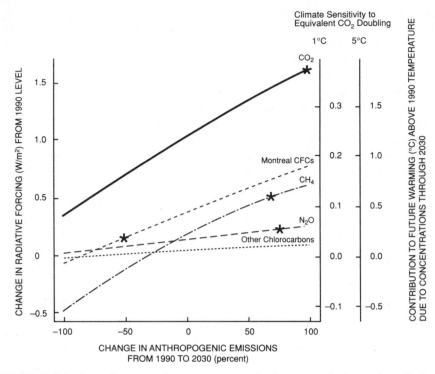

FIGURE 3.4 Commitment to future warming. An incremental change in radiative forcing between 1990 and 2030 due to emissions of greenhouse gases implies a change in global average equilibrium temperature (see text). The scales on the right-hand side show two ranges of global average temperature responses. The first corresponds to a climate whose temperature response to an equivalent of doubling of the preindustrial level of CO_2 is 1°C; the second corresponds to a rise of 5°C for an equivalent doubling of CO_2. These scales indicate the equilibrium commitment to future warming caused by emissions from 1990 through 2030. Assumptions are as in Figure 3.2.

To determine equilibrium warming in 2030 due to continued emissions of CO_2 at the 1990 level, find the point on the curve labeled "CO_2" that is vertically above 0 percent change on the bottom scale. The equilibrium warming on the right-hand scales is about 0.23°C (0.4°F) for a climate system with 1° sensitivity and about 1.2°C (2.2°F) for a system with 5° sensitivity. For CH_4 emissions continuing at 1990 levels through 2030, the equilibrium warming would be about 0.04°C (0.07°F) at 1° sensitivity and about 0.25°C (0.5°F) at 5° sensitivity. These steps must be repeated for each gas. Total warming associated with 1990-level emissions of the gases shown until 2030 would be about 0.41°C (0.7°F) at 1° sensitivity and about 2.2°C (4°F) at 5° sensitivity.

Scenarios of changes in committed future warming accompanying different greenhouse gas emission rates can be constructed by repeating this process for given emission rates and adding up the results.

ture is reached. In an equilibrium condition, all of the incoming energy is radiated back to space. During the transient period, however, some of that incoming heat is still being used to heat up the deep oceans, which warm more slowly than the atmosphere. So the surface temperature of the planet is not yet at the temperature required to balance all of the incoming energy. Accordingly, the full commitment to temperature rise corresponding to the greenhouse gas accumulations at a given time may not become fully apparent for several decades (or more). The ultimate increase in global average temperature corresponding to a given increase in greenhouse gas concentration is called the equilibrium global average temperature.

Figure 3.4 shows possible impacts on the global equilibrium temperature of changes in atmospheric concentrations of greenhouse gases. Two scales have been added to the right-hand side of the figure describing the radiative forcing properties of greenhouse gases (Figure 3.2). The scale labeled 5°C is associated with the hypothesis that the equivalent of doubling CO_2 would produce a 5° increase in the equilibrium global average temperature, and the 1°C scale accompanies the hypothesis that such a doubling would imply a 1° increase.

Figure 3.4 can be used to construct scenarios of changes in committed future warming resulting from policies that lead to different greenhouse gas emission rates. In particular, it can be used to produce a first approximation of the implications for greenhouse warming of policies resulting in specified emission rates. This could be very helpful in establishing priorities for action. For example, the effect of reducing N_2O emissions by 10 percent is much smaller than that of reducing CH_4 by 10 percent.

Because it is so difficult to determine the extent of global warming from temperature measurements alone, it would be very helpful to monitor the radiation balance of the earth. There are currently, however, no functioning satellites capable of directly measuring outbound infrared radiation.

WHAT WE CAN LEARN FROM CLIMATE MODELS

The climate is extremely variable. Temperature, humidity, precipitation, and wind vary markedly from week to week and season to season. These natural variations are commonly much larger than the changes associated with greenhouse warming. There are also patterns to these natural variations, and it is these patterns that we think of as "climate."

The importance of greenhouse warming will be determined by the magnitude and abruptness of the associated climatic changes. Useful prediction requires credible quantitative estimates of those changes. Numerical computer simulations using general circulation models (GCMs) are generally considered the best available tools for anticipating climatic changes. Data from previous interglacial periods can be compared to results from computer models. Past conditions, however, are inexact metaphors for current increases in atmospheric concentrations of trace gases.

In order to simulate the intricate climatic system, GCMs themselves are complicated. They are complex computational schemes incorporating well-established scientific laws, empirical knowledge, and implicit representations. Mechanisms occurring on scales smaller than the smallest elements of the atmosphere, land, or oceans resolved in the GCM (i.e., "subgrid" scales) are represented by mathematical characterizations called "parameterizations." A typical GCM involves hundreds of thousands of equations and dozens of variables. About half a dozen different model types exist, and others are being developed.

One major drawback common to all current GCMs is that they lack adequately validated representations of important factors like cloud cover feedback, ocean circulation, and hydrologic interactions. Therefore it is unreasonable to expect the models to provide precise predictions, decades into the future, of global average temperature. This is especially so given that the expected global temperature rise is smaller than current naturally occurring regional temperature fluctuations on all time scales, daily, seasonal, and decadal.

General circulation models most commonly simulate the equilibrium climatic conditions associated with doubling atmospheric concentrations of CO_2 compared to preindustrial levels. Current GCM simulations based on these assumptions show a range of global average equilibrium temperature increases of 1.9° to 5.2°C (3.4° to 9.4°F). Many other calculations and simulations have been conducted; some with no cloud interactions, some with only a simple heat sink in place of oceans, some with no distinction between day and night. For the most part, these calculations also provide predictions within or close to this range.

The GCM results have been interpreted in slightly different ways by groups with differing perspectives. The Intergovernmental Panel on Climate Change (IPCC) used a range of 2° to 4°C (3.6° to 7.2°F) accompanying an equivalent doubling of preindustrial CO_2. The National Research Council's Board on Atmospheric Sciences and Climate used a range of 1.5° to 4.5°C (2.7° to 8.1°F), numbers receiving slightly greater usage among atmospheric scientists.

For the purposes of informed policy choice, it is crucial to acknowledge the limited capability of the GCMs. This is especially true because there is no clear connection between temperature records of the last century and the atmospheric accumulation of greenhouse gases. The temperature record for the northern hemisphere, for example, shows some rise until about 1940, a slight decrease from 1940 until the mid-1970s, followed by another rise. There currently is no persuasive evidence that these variations were driven by growing atmospheric concentrations of greenhouse gases. The 100-year temperature record is not inconsistent with the range of climate sensitivity predicted by the GCMs, but neither is it inconsistent with the natural variability of the earth's climate.

There is another key limitation on the knowledge acquired from GCMs. In essence there are fewer than two dozen GCM simulation runs with five independent models on which to base conclusions. Every one incorporates untested and unvalidated hypotheses. They may be sensitive to changes in ways that current calculations have not yet revealed. For example, a recent examination of available computer runs shows considerable difference in the treatment of clouds. Although all runs yield similar results for a "clear sky" without clouds, their results vary substantially when clouds are included. The limited number of GCM simulations has two important consequences. First, there are too few runs to scientifically determine "most likely" values within the range. Second, it is not strictly possible to eliminate temperature changes of less than 1°C (1.8°F) or greater than 5°C (9°F).

Although GCMs cannot produce scientific "proof" in their predictions, they do map seasonal cycles of surface temperature quite well. GCMs also reasonably simulate daily and annual variability in air pressure patterns over large areas. In addition, most models represent the broad features of wind patterns, and the most recent models provide realistic simulations of winter and summer jet streams in the lower stratosphere. GCM simulations of other climate variables, such as precipitation, soil moisture, and north-south energy transport, are much less satisfactory. They do not provide credible quantitative estimates of the longer-term changes in global climate that might be driven by greenhouse gas accumulations.

The panel believes that prudent policy choices should be based on conservative assumptions in the face of large uncertainty. The panel uses a range of 1° to 5°C (1.8° to 9°F) and notes that it is broader than ranges adopted by other groups. In the panel's view, this range expresses much less unwarranted faith in the numbers produced by GCMs than does a narrower range.

Simply looking at the global average temperature associated with an equivalent doubling of preindustrial levels of CO_2 does not convey some important aspects of climate change. For example, there is no particular significance to exactly that level of greenhouse gas concentrations. In fact, unless serious efforts to limit releases of greenhouse gases are undertaken, atmospheric concentrations will exceed this level during the next century. In addition, GCMs may not produce reliable information about regional or local aspects of climate change that are of greatest interest to decision makers. These include amounts and timing of precipitation, frequency and timing of floods and temperature extremes, and wind extremes. Soil moisture content, dates of first and last frost, and timing of exceptionally hot days are all more important for plant life than is average temperature.

WHAT WE CAN LEARN FROM THE
TEMPERATURE RECORD

Global temperature data are available for the period 1890 to 1990, but those from the earlier half of the century are difficult to interpret with confidence. The most comprehensive assessment of the record of surface temperature, depicted in Figure 3.5, reveals a warming since the late nineteenth century of between 0.3° and 0.6°C (0.5° and 1.1°F). This warming is supported by several different kinds of information. Adjustments have been attempted to negate known complicating factors such as the biases introduced by the location of long-term measurement stations near urban areas with their attendant local warming.

To some extent the natural temperature variation in the climatic system makes it difficult to interpret the observational record. In particular, it is not possible to determine how much, if any, of the average global temperature rise over the last century might be attributed to greenhouse warming.

Increasing atmospheric concentrations of greenhouse gases may produce changes in both the magnitude and the rate of change of global average temperature that have few or no precedents in the earth's recent history. Figure 3.6 depicts estimates of the ranges of temperature in various periods of the past. A range of less than 1°C (1.8°F) was experienced in the last century, less than 2°C (3.6°F) in the last 10,000 years, and perhaps 7°C (13°F) in the last million years. Figure 3.6 shows these temperatures compared to a line representing an average global temperature of about 15°C (59°F), which is the global average temperature for the period 1951 to 1980. During this period the largest number of temperature recording stations were operating, and the averages for this period are commonly used as a base against which to assess global temperatures. Despite the modest decline in the average temperature in the northern hemisphere between about 1940 and 1975, we are still in an unusually warm period of earth's history. Thus the temperature increases of a few degrees projected for the next century are not only large in recent historical terms, but could also carry the planet into largely unknown territory.

Recent analyses, however, raise the possibility that some greenhouse warming could be offset by the cooling effect of sulfate aerosol emissions. Such emissions may have contributed to regional temperature variations and to differences in the temperature records of the northern and southern hemispheres.

On the geologic time scale, many things affect climate in addition to trace gases in the atmosphere: changes in solar output, changes in the earth's orbital path, changes in land and ocean distribution, changes in the reflectivity of the earth, and cataclysmic events like meteor impacts or extended volcanic eruptions.

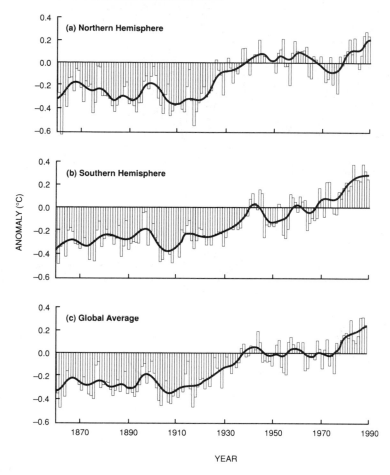

FIGURE 3.5 Combined land air and sea surface temperature relative to 1951-1980 average temperatures. Land air temperatures are typically measured 1 to 2 m above ground level. Sea surface temperatures are typically measured in the layer from the ocean's surface to several meters below.

SOURCES: Land air temperatures are updated from P. D. Jones, S. C. B. Raper, R. S. Bradley, H. F. Diaz, P. M. Kelly, and T. M. L. Wigley. 1986. Southern hemisphere surface air temperature variations, 1851-1984. *Journal of Climate and Applied Meteorology* 25:1213-1230. P. D. Jones, S. C. B. Raper, R. S. Bradley, H. F. Diaz, P. M. Kelly, and T. M. L. Wigley. 1986. Northern hemisphere surface air temperature variations, 1851-1984. *Journal of Climate and Applied Meteorology* 25:161-179. Sea surface temperatures are from the U.K. Meteorological Office and the COADS as adjusted by G. Farmer, T. M. L. Wigley, P. D. Jones, and M. Salmon. 1989. Documenting and explaining recent global-mean temperature changes. *Final Report to NERC,* Contract GR/3/6565. Norwich, United Kingdom: Climate Research Unit.

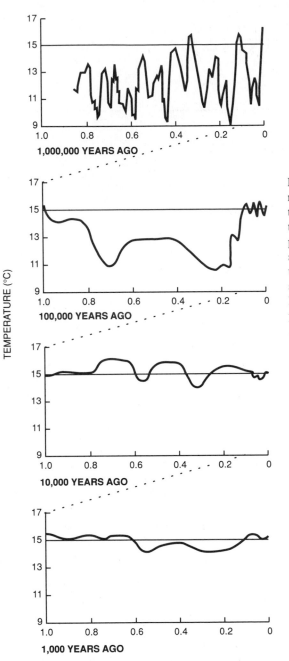

FIGURE 3.6 An approximate temperature history of the northern hemisphere for the last 850,000 years. The panels are at the same vertical scale. The top panel shows the last million years, the second panel amplifies the last 100,000 years, the third panel the last 10,000 years, and the bottom panel the last 1,000 years. The horizontal line at 15°C is included for reference and is the approximate average global temperature for the period 1951 to 1980. Considerable uncertainty attaches to the record in each panel, and the temperature records are derived from a variety of sources, for example, ice volume, as well as more direct data. Spatial and temporal (e.g., seasonal) variation of data sources is also considerable.

SOURCE: National Research Council. 1983. *Changing Climate: Report of the Carbon Dioxide Assessment Committee.* Washington, D.C.: National Academy Press. Figure 1.14.

These and other contributors to the earth's climate make it difficult to interpret the temperature history. Just as it is impossible to rule out natural variability, it is also impossible to rule out an underlying trend, so that the observed rise of 0.3° to 0.6°C (0.5° to 1.1°F) may be superimposed on a long-term (but nonuniform) rise or fall in global temperature.

SEA LEVEL

Average sea level of the oceans has varied throughout earth's history, and it is changing slightly today. Global sea level was about 100 m (328 feet) lower than current levels at the coldest point of the last ice age about 18,000 years ago. During the geologic past, there have been repeated variations from present sea level of more than this amount, both during times of intense glaciation and during periods in which the earth was free of ice. All of human civilization, however, has lived in a period when the average sea level was roughly as it is today.

Tide gauges measure sea level variations in relation to a fixed point on land and thus record "relative sea level" (RSL). RSL at any particular place varies over time and space. The direct causes of these variations include vertical motions of land to which the tide gauge or other measuring device is attached and changes in the volume of sea water in which the gauge is immersed. Differences in atmospheric pressure, water runoff from land, winds, ocean currents, and the density of sea water all cause variations in sea level in comparison to the global average sea surface.

Climate-related contributions to sea level change are of two kinds: variations in the actual amount or mass of water in the ocean basins (due mostly to changes in precipitation and runoff) and thermal expansion or contraction (changes in the density of water, due to variations of temperature and salinity).

The melting of the northern continental ice sheets between 15,000 and 7,000 years before the present probably accounts for most of the rise of the sea to present levels. Some have suggested that global warming due to increased atmospheric concentrations of greenhouse gases could lead to disintegration of the West Antarctic Ice Sheet, most of which is grounded below sea level. If climate warms and warmer ocean water intrudes under the ice sheet, the release of ice from the sheet would accelerate. The melting of the West Antarctic Ice Sheet is quite unlikely, however, and virtually impossible by the end of the next century. Estimates based on a combined oceanic and atmospheric GCM suggest that several hundred years would be required to achieve this amount of warming. The principal effects on sea level of greenhouse warming over the time period examined in this study will thus be due to thermal expansion.

Thermal expansion (and contraction) of the oceans, caused by a combination of increasing (decreasing) temperature and salinity, accounts for seasonal and interannual variations in sea level. These changes are not large enough, however, to account for the differences over tens of thousands of years. Warming the entire ocean from 0°C (32°F) to the current global average ocean temperature would result in a thermal expansion of about 10 m (33 feet).

In order to estimate oceanic thermal expansion from greenhouse warming, changes in the temperature, salinity, and density of the oceans have to be considered. Two types of models yield somewhat different results, depending on the assumptions made concerning transfer of heat into the deep ocean waters. The results are 20 to 110 cm (8 to 43 inches) when heat is carried downward by eddy diffusion and 10 to 50 cm (4 to 20 inches) when some downward diffusion is balanced by upwelling from the deep oceans. Both estimates are for the year 2100 and an equivalent of doubling the preindustrial atmospheric concentration of CO_2. The panel used a range of sea level rise from 0 to 60 cm (24 inches) for a doubling of CO_2.

POSSIBLE DRAMATIC CHANGES

The behavior of complex and poorly understood systems can easily surprise even the most careful observer. There are many aspects of the climate system that we do not understand well and which could provide such surprises. In particular, some radical changes that could result from increases in global temperatures must be considered plausible even though our understanding of them is not sufficient to analyze their magnitudes or likelihoods:

1. CH_4 could be released as high-latitude tundra melts, providing a sudden increase of CH_4, which would add to greenhouse warming.
2. The combination of increased runoff of fresh water in high latitudes and a reduced temperature differential from equator to pole could result in radically changed major ocean currents leading to altered weather patterns.
3. There could be a significant melting of the West Antarctic Ice Sheet, resulting in a sea level several meters higher than it is today.

Such major (and perhaps rapid) changes could be accompanied by more dramatic warming of the atmospheric and oceanic systems than is now apparent. No credible claim can be made that any of these events is imminent: nonetheless, with continuing greenhouse gas accumulations, none of them are precluded.

CONCLUSIONS

Neither the available climate record nor the limited capabilities of the climate models permit a reliable forecast of the implications of continued accumulations of greenhouse gases in the atmosphere. Neither do they permit an assessment as to whether the increase from 1890 to 1990 in global average temperature can be attributed to greenhouse gases. However, it is probable that some positive rate of warming will accompany continued accumulation of greenhouse gases in the atmosphere. An important question is: When will we have a more definite fix on the rate at which warming will occur?

It is unlikely that our understanding of such basic phenomena as the role of clouds and ocean dynamics will improve greatly over the next few years. It is also unlikely that a useful level of improvement in regional predictive capability will emerge in that time. A few decades may be required before atmospheric scientists produce the answers we seek. Some current limitations on our knowledge could be reduced by better characterization of such "subgrid" processes as precipitation and mechanical heat transfer, better coupling of atmospheric, land surface, and oceanic models, and better models of the role of ecosystems. Access to computers with greater capacity and speed would accelerate these improvements. All of these depend in large measure on progress in the scientific understanding on which the models are based.

The overall magnitude of greenhouse warming and its rate of emergence can only be inferred from several different kinds of information. The pieces of the puzzle are currently understood with varying degrees of uncertainty. Nevertheless, there is clear evidence and wide agreement among atmospheric scientists about several basic facts:

1. The atmospheric concentration of CO_2 has increased 25 percent during the last century and is currently increasing at about 0.5 percent per year.

2. The atmospheric concentration of CH_4 has doubled during that period and is increasing at about 0.9 percent per year.

3. CFCs, which are man-made and have been released into the atmosphere in quantity only since World War II, are currently increasing at about 4 percent per year.

4. Items 1, 2, and 3 are primarily direct consequences of human activities.

5. Current interpretations of temperature records reveal that the global average temperature has increased between 0.3° and 0.6°C (0.5° and 1.1°F) during the last century.

As a result, the panel concludes that there is a reasonable chance of the following:

1. In the absence of greater human effort to the contrary, greenhouse gas concentrations equivalent to a doubling of the preindustrial level of CO_2 will occur by the middle of the next century.

2. The sensitivity of the climatic system to greenhouse gases is such that the equivalent of doubling CO_2 could ultimately increase the average global temperature by somewhere between 1° and 5°C (1.8° and 9°F).

3. The transfer of heat to the deep oceans occurs more slowly than within the atmosphere or the upper layers of the ocean. The resulting transient period, or "lag," means that the global average surface temperature at any time is lower than the temperature that would prevail after all the redistribution had been completed. At the time of equivalent CO_2 doubling, for example, the global average surface temperature may be as little as one-half the ultimate equilibrium temperature associated with those concentrations.

4. A rise of sea level may accompany global warming, possibly in the range of 0 to 60 cm (0 to 24 inches) for the temperature range listed above.

5. Several troublesome, possibly dramatic, repercussions of continued increases in global temperature have been suggested. No credible claim can be made that any of these events is imminent, but none of them are precluded.

4

Policy Framework

The previous chapter clearly points out gaps in our knowledge and understanding of key physical phenomena in greenhouse warming. Nevertheless, current scientific knowledge seems to indicate that unconstrained releases of greenhouse gases from fossil fuel combustion and other sources would ultimately cause climate change. There are no specific conclusions, however, about the regional and local effects associated with increased atmospheric concentrations of greenhouse gases. Nor is there much indication about how rapidly the effects might emerge.

Our knowledge about other topics central to the analysis of the greenhouse warming problem is at least as insecure. The number of analyses of the overall impact on the economy of this country of greenhouse warming is even smaller than the number of GCM runs simulating an equivalent doubling of CO_2. Economic experts differ in their assumptions about future population and economic growth, technological change, and a host of other factors. Because the economic models must project trends far into the future, their results are likely to remain controversial.

How then, in the midst of this uncertainty, can we begin to evaluate policy options? Several concepts that can help us in that task are presented in the next two sections.

COMPARING MITIGATION AND ADAPTATION

Many different policies could be adopted in response to the prospect of greenhouse warming. In order to evaluate these policy options, it is useful to categorize them into three types:

1. Options that eliminate or reduce greenhouse gas emissions.

2. Options that "offset" emissions by removing greenhouse gases from the atmosphere, by blocking incident solar radiation, or by altering the reflection or absorption properties of the earth's surface.

3. Options that help human and ecologic systems adjust or adapt to new climatic conditions and events.

In this report the first and second types of interventions are referred to as "mitigation" since they can take effect prior to the onset of climate change and slow its pace. Mitigation options are discussed in more detail in Chapter 6. The third type of intervention is referred to as "adaptation" since its effects come into play primarily after climate has changed. A fuller discussion of adaptation appears in Chapter 5.

In comparing mitigation and adaptation, one consideration is whether a given action will, in addition to providing adaptation or mitigation benefits, also improve economic efficiency. Even progressive societies find much of their economic activity falling short of demonstrated "best practice." New, more efficient practices are being developed continually, but it takes time for them to diffuse throughout the economy. There are many obstacles to more rapid diffusion of better practice, including lack of information, insufficient supply of components or products, political interests, inappropriate incentives, and simple human inertia. In general, however, every society has many opportunities to improve its overall situation by reducing the gap between current practice and best practice. Many of the actions taken to deal with potential greenhouse warming could also improve economic well-being because they are more efficient than prevailing practice. These options should be distinguished from another class of actions: so-called "free-standing" actions, which satisfy other social or environmental objectives (and may or may not contribute to economic efficiency as such).

Figure 4.1 compares hypothetical mitigation and adaptation actions in response to potential greenhouse warming. If climate change occurs, and no mitigation or adaptation actions are undertaken, a substantial reduction in real income is likely over time. Initially, mitigation is likely to reduce real income more than either doing nothing or taking adaptation measures as climatic changes emerge. Ultimately, however, mitigation actions could result in higher real income than waiting and taking adaptation measures. In this scenario, investing in mitigation reduces consumption now, but produces advantages in the future. Expenditures on mitigation options should thus be seen as investments in the future.

Many combinations of mitigation and adaptation actions are possible. Choosing the best mix of mitigation and adaptation strategies depends in part on the discount rate applied to the investment. The higher the discount rate, the greater the case for postponement of costly actions. Use of discount rates is one way of assigning values to future outcomes.

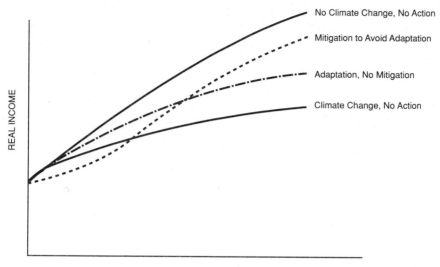

FIGURE 4.1 Schematic comparison of mitigation and adaptation. The uppermost curve plots world economic well-being, essentially the amount of real income available for consumption, assuming that there is no climate change. The lowest curve plots world economic well-being assuming that there is climate change and no actions are taken either to prevent or to cope with those changes. Notice that the axes are not defined quantitatively. Thus the curves are only relative, and this figure cannot be used to estimate the amount of economic welfare lost by expenditures on mitigation. Similarly, it cannot be used to estimate the time at which the return from expenditures on mitigation would exceed the return from expenditures on adaptation.

ASSIGNING VALUES TO FUTURE OUTCOMES

Most people have a time preference for money. They would rather have, for example, $100 to use today than $105 a year from now. Future costs and benefits are usually transformed into their "present value" by using a discount rate, which is similar to the interest on savings. Discount rates enable current and future returns to be compared.

A central, and controversial, issue is which discount rate to use in weighing the relative advantages of present and future impacts and costs. There are essentially three courses of action with regard to responding to potential greenhouse warming: (1) we can invest resources now to slow greenhouse gas emissions; (2) we can invest in other projects that might yield a higher return; and (3) we can defer any kind of investment in the future in favor of current consumption. Applying a discount rate near the yield on other investments—at least 10 percent per year in most countries, in real terms—

in evaluating responses to greenhouse warming would lead to the conclusion that our investment dollars could be most efficiently used in capital projects, education, or other sectors. It suggests that we should not take costly, low-payoff actions to reduce greenhouse gas emissions. High discount rates place a low value on future outcomes. Applying a low discount rate to greenhouse investment choices—say, 3 percent per year—would make investing now to avoid greenhouse warming more attractive. But such a low discount rate means that other investment opportunities have been exhausted or are being ignored. It is likely that there will be more investment opportunities with returns of greater than 3 percent than there are available funds. A low discount rate on resources invested in response to potential climate change is inconsistent with a high return on capital investment.

The panel makes no attempt to resolve this issue. This study uses rates of 3, 6, and 10 percent in calculations to ensure that unique circumstances that would alter assessment of the outcome are not overlooked. Because consumers sometimes act in ways that indicate an even higher discount rate in their purchases, a rate of 30 percent is also used in considering some mitigation options. For the purposes of comparing options and arriving at recommendations for action, the panel used a single real discount rate of 6 percent per year. Use of a 10 percent discount rate would decrease the present value of the low-cost options but would not change their rankings.

A METHOD FOR COMPARING OPTIONS

Using the concepts described above, we can compare options by care-fully enumerating the impacts of action and inaction and then trying to find a course that minimizes the net costs of the impacts of mitigation and adaptation.

More specifically, the anticipated consequences of greenhouse warming (both adverse and beneficial) can be arrayed to produce a "damage function" showing the anticipated costs and benefits associated with projected climatic changes. The mitigation and adaptation options can be similarly arrayed according to what they would cost and how effective they would be. A well-designed response will involve balancing incremental impacts and costs. A sensible policy requires that the level of action chosen be "cost-effective," which means that the total cost of attaining a level of reduction of climate change should be minimized.

Ideally, the evaluation would consider the full costs associated with each mitigation alternative. Called "full social cost pricing," such an analysis would allocate to each option not only the costs of its development, construction, operation, and decommissioning or disposal, but also those of environmental or health problems resulting from its use. Burning coal, for example, not only emits greenhouse gases, but also contributes to a variety of health problems (for nearby residents as well as coal miners) and to environmental problems such as acid rain. All these would be included in full social cost pricing. A different example involves increasing automobile fuel efficiency by reducing the size and weight of vehicles. Reducing vehicle size results both in reduced emissions of greenhouse gases, a benefit, and in increased likelihood of injury from collisions with larger vehicles, a cost. Ideally, all costs and benefits would be considered.

In practice, such a framework can be used only in an approximate manner. It is impossible to determine all of the costs of all options today, much less of climatic changes that will not occur for 50 to 100 years. Many of the important concerns are difficult to measure and are not fully captured in prices or other market indicators. Nevertheless, the panel finds this conceptual framework to be a constructive way to organize the evaluation of policy options.

Assessing Mitigation Options

Most mitigation options considered here use currently available techniques and equipment that could be installed within 10 years. Actions that reduce or offset emissions of greenhouse gases or otherwise deal with greenhouse warming are evaluated in terms of annualized costs and annualized reduction of CO_2 emissions. Options addressing greenhouse gases other than CO_2 are translated into the equivalent CO_2 emissions. Annualized costs (or emissions) are determined by estimating the total costs in constant dollars (or emissions in CO_2 equivalent) of that option over its lifetime. This includes the so-called "engineering" costs of construction, installation, operation, maintenance, and decommissioning or disposal. The total discounted cost is divided by the number of years the option is expected to last, resulting in the annualized cost of that option. Annualized emission reductions are calculated in a similar fashion.

The mitigation options in this menu are then ranked according to their cost-effectiveness. Those achieving the reduction of CO_2 or CO_2-equivalent emissions most cheaply are ranked highest. Finally, the overall potential of each option is estimated because there are limits on how much can be achieved with each option. For example, avoiding emissions by using hydroelectric power generation might be comparatively cheap, but there are few remaining locations in the United States where dams could be built. Its overall potential is therefore relatively small.

This method has distinct advantages and disadvantages. One advantage is that it enables options with different lifetimes to be compared. The costs (and benefits) of a natural gas-fired electricity plant may accrue over 25 to 30 years, a much longer period than the periods associated with vehicle efficiency improvements, since the typical life of a car is probably not more than 10 years. A disadvantage is that because implementation of the high-priority options would change the pattern of emissions over time, the cost-effectiveness of various options during the later portion of their operating life might be different. For example, programs to use electricity more efficiently appear quite cost-effective in the panel's current analysis. If such programs were aggressively implemented, the need for new electricity generating capacity over the next few decades would be reduced. Thus the cost-effectiveness of investments in power generation in, say, 2010 could be altered by electricity conservation programs today. This study makes no attempt to account for such possibilities, but they could be examined in future studies.

Each time a new analysis is performed, a new series of "least cost" options will emerge. This circumstance allows policymakers to regularly adjust actions to ensure the most efficient use of resources.

Assessing Adaptation Options

Options intended to help people and unmanaged systems of plants and animals adapt to future climate change are more difficult to assess than mitigation programs. First, we must speculate about future climatic conditions. GCMs are currently unable to accurately predict local and regional events and conditions of greatest interest to policymakers.

Second, we must predict how the affected systems are likely to react to the changing conditions. Sensitivity to climate change depends on many things, including physiological response to temperature or moisture stress and dependency on other components of the system. A crucial concept in the assessment is the speed at which the system adjusts. If adjustments are made more rapidly than climatic conditions change, the system should be able to adapt without government assistance, although not without cost.

In the panel's analysis of adaptation options, "benchmark" costs were developed on the basis of the costs of contemporary extreme weather events or conservation and restoration programs. These estimates were used to develop a measure of the magnitude of the costs that might be associated with climate change.

But the panel recognizes that many issues cannot be quantified. This is especially true for impacts, and the impacts of concern are of three fundamentally different kinds.

First are the consequences, either beneficial or harmful, for things that are exchanged in markets. Agriculture, for example, will be affected by changes in precipitation patterns and dates of frost in ways that will be captured in prices and other market indicators. These are reasonably easy to quantify, and adding up the market effects gives a clear picture of the impacts.

Second are things whose values are not well captured in markets. Genetic resources are generally undervalued because there are few property rights in genetic resources and people therefore cannot capture the benefits of the investments they might make in preserving biodiversity. Many species are unlikely ever to have marketable attributes, and it is virtually impossible to predict which ones may ultimately have economic value. These consequences are not well identified in current accounting systems.

Third are items that some people value for reasons that have little to do with their "usefulness" or economic worth. This "ecocentric" valuation assigns intrinsic value to the living world. Species loss, in this view, is undesirable regardless of any economic value that may derive from those species. Humanity, it is held, should not do things that alter the course of natural evolution.

The panel recognizes the difficulty of measuring these noneconomic criteria in the quantitative method described above. Since such values are codified, to some extent, in laws (e.g., those to protect biodiversity), potential greenhouse warming responses must be consistent with protection of the noneconomic values. These may be among the most difficult values to accommodate if climates change substantially. In spite of the difficulties outlined above, the panel believes this cost-effectiveness approach is the most useful method for evaluating policies involving response to greenhouse warming.

OTHER FACTORS AFFECTING POLICY CHOICES ABOUT GREENHOUSE WARMING

Once policy options have been ranked, certain factors not directly related to greenhouse warming come into play in the decision-making process.

One such factor concerns risk perception. People differ in their willingness to take risks. We can expect people to differ in their reaction to the potential and uncertain threat of greenhouse warming as well. Some people may be distressed by the possibility that cherished parts of their cultural heritage or natural landscapes might be lost. Others might be unwilling to accept some aspects of proposed adjustments—perhaps abandoning their traditional homeland and moving elsewhere. In any case, people and organizations will differ in their judgments about how much society should pay to reduce the chance of uncertain climate change.

Another factor is the constraint of limited resources. The United States is a large, wealthy country. Many other nations are severely constrained in their ability to act because of limited financial and human resources.

5

Adaptation

The amount of money, labor, and equipment we are willing to expend to avoid greenhouse warming depends in part on how we view the results of climate change and how much we are willing to risk possible negative consequences. Estimating all these outcomes is difficult, however, because we cannot predict with certainty what changes will occur globally and we cannot predict at all the effects in a given region. Regardless of what the changes will be, a necessary first step in determining the proper allocation of resources is to examine the ability of natural systems and humans to adapt.

METHODS OF ADAPTATION

Humans, animals, and plants are able to adapt to different climates. Animals and plants live in the Himalayas and in Death Valley, although not all species thrive in both. Human adaptability is shown by our living and working in both Riyadh and Barrow.

Human societies can and do thrive in many different climates, but it is the rate of climate change as much as its magnitude that could pose a threat. Disasters caused by severe weather and degradation of the environment illustrate the kinds of disruptions that could accompany rapid climate change. There are five alternative human responses: (1) modify the hazard, as by channeling rivers that are prone to flooding; (2) prevent or limit impacts, as by building dikes; (3) move or avoid the loss, as by implementing flood plain zoning; (4) share the loss, as by providing insurance; and (5) bear the loss, as by losing all or part of a crop. Thus we have a large menu of potential adaptation options, some of which are best made before an event and some after.

Plants and animals will always be found regardless of climatic changes in the ranges discussed here. The threat to the natural communities of plants and animals, called ecosystems, from greenhouse warming also comes from its projected rate of change as much as its magnitude. If the climate changes as rapidly as some computer models project, the present natural ecosystems may become fragmented and break up. New communities may replace them with different mixes of species. Long-lived plants like trees, for example, might persist. If ill adapted to the new conditions, however, they would fail to compete and reproduce. Species better fitted to the new climate would immigrate, sometimes hastened by disturbances of various kinds. Species well suited to the changing conditions may become more dominant, or pioneer species that could fill a particular niche may thrive in the new conditions. Certain ecosystems might vanish if the climate that currently sustains them disappears or changes its location faster than the key species are able to migrate.

THE ROLE OF INNOVATION

Much human adaptation involves the invention and diffusion of technological "hardware" or "software." Examples of technological hardware include air conditioners that make hot days comfortable and tractors that cultivate large tracts of land in a few days if spring is late. Software includes information, rules, and procedures like weather forecasts or insurance restrictions. Knowledge and new procedures are generally indispensable for adopting new hardware. Major breakthroughs like irrigation usually consist of innovations in social organization and financing as well as new machinery.

Many past innovations in hardware and software have helped people adapt themselves and their activities to climate and variable weather. Food preservation in warm weather, refrigeration and air conditioning, antifreeze for all-weather automobile travel, and weather satellites to aid prediction all help. Such innovations can occur rapidly in comparison to the 40 to 50 years envisioned for the equivalent doubling of atmospheric CO_2. For example, in 1900 California had little crop production; in 1985 it produced twice as many dollars of crops as second-place Iowa. Penicillin was discovered in 1928; by 1945 it was saving thousands of lives.

The question frequently asked is how rapidly inventions can replace existing equipment and how fast other technology can be supplanted. About two-thirds of capital stock in most industrialized countries is in machinery, and one-third is in buildings and other structures. This capital stock turns over more rapidly than might be expected. Most current office space, for example, is in buildings built in the last 20 years. In Japan, the average period for virtually complete replacement of machinery and equipment ranges from about 22 years in textiles to about 10 years in industries like telecommunications or electrical machinery. Replacement can be fast in agriculture, too. The estimated lifetime of particular strains for five major crops in the United States is less than 10 years and is expected to be even shorter in the future.

As societies have become more affluent, they have reduced their sensitivity to natural phenomena in many ways. Overall, the trend is toward systems of transportation, communication, and energy production and use that are less sensitive to climate. Improved technology and social organization also seem to have lessened the impacts of climate fluctuations on food supply over the last 100 years. In the time frame over which the effects of greenhouse warming are felt, more societies may become more robust with respect to climate change.

ASSESSING IMPACTS AND ADAPTIVE CAPACITY

The data and analyses used in this study to assess impacts and adaptive capacity are drawn mostly, but not exclusively, from the United States. Few other countries share the United States' combination of wealth, low population density, and range of climates. Moreover, the panel recognizes that our domestic well-being is intimately tied to what happens in other countries. Major international shifts in trade flows, agricultural production, energy demand patterns, and more could profoundly affect this country. But a full analysis of such global interactions remains for future studies.

The assessment of impacts in this study examines separately the sensitivity of various human and ecologic systems to climate change. Not all interactions could be assessed, even though the panel recognizes that such interactions may be relevant. For example, unmanaged natural systems have important interactions with forestry. Although the assessment of forestry considers shifts in ranges of pests and other key species, major alterations in unmanaged natural systems may contain unforeseen problems for forestry. The assessment here is an initial appraisal of impacts and adaptive capabilities of affected human and natural systems in the United States; additional effort is necessary for a more complete understanding of these issues.

CO_2 Fertilization of Green Plants

An increasing atmospheric concentration of CO_2 would increase agricultural production by enhancing the use of sunlight and slowing transpiration in some plants. The overall production of organic material also depends on other factors such as temperature, moisture, and nutrients. It is difficult to anticipate the amount of increased organic production accompanying greenhouse warming because extrapolation from small-scale laboratory experiments to whole fields of crops or to complete systems of unmanaged plants and animals is uncertain. The increases in photosynthesis and slowing of transpiration, however, would probably be somewhat less than observed in laboratory experiments. These effects would apply to plants in agriculture, managed forests, and unmanaged ecosystems.

Agriculture

Changes in average temperature are probably less important for agricultural productivity than changes in precipitation and evaporation. Whether the projected changes are calculated as precipitation and evaporation or the resulting changes in crop yields, the different climate scenarios produced by different general circulation models (GCMs) yield large variations for agriculture. But farming has always been sensitive to the weather, and experience suggests that farmers adapt quickly, especially in comparison to the rate at which greenhouse warming would occur. Countries like the United States, which encompass many climate zones and have active and aggressive agricultural research and development, would probably be able to adapt their farming to climatic changes deriving from greenhouse warming. Poorer countries with less wealth or fewer climate zones may have more difficulty avoiding problems or taking advantage of better conditions.

Managed Forests and Grasslands

Forests and grasslands each cover more than a quarter of the United States. Trees have long lifetimes, and are unlikely to adjust rapidly enough by themselves to accommodate rapid warming. Forests, however, can be managed to preserve ample forest products. Middle-aged forests are at most risk if climate changes, since young forests can be replaced cheaply and older ones are valuable to sustain. The adaptation of valuable forests by management is possible using methods that are flexible and work in many climates.

Natural Landscape

The natural landscape consists of unmanaged ecosystems that include many species of animals, plants, and microorganisms harvested as game, fruit, or drugs. Ecosystems absorb CO_2, emit O_2, and cleanse air and water. Ecosystems also emit CO_2, CH_4, and other hydrocarbons. For a variety of reasons, the adaptation of natural ecosystems to climate change is more problematic than that of managed systems like farms or plantation forests. The principal impacts of climate change are expected to be on plants. Impacts on animals would mostly be indirect, through changes in plant functioning and vegetation dynamics, but significant direct effects of climate change are possible. Some species of birds appear especially responsive to temperature and may shift their ranges relatively rapidly. Climate change may make some species extinct, but the diversity of ecosystems would probably protect those functions that are carried out by many species. For example, diseases removed first the chestnut and then the elm from eastern forests, but the loss of their capacity to absorb CO_2 was quickly made up by other species. Some ecological processes, however, are carried out by only a few species. Only a few species enhance soil productivity by fixing nitrogen, and the grazing of a single large species may alter a landscape. If climate change removed one of these species or encouraged another, even a diverse ecosystem could be affected. Even small climatic changes resulting from greenhouse warming would be likely to alter unmanaged ecosystems. The adaptation of the natural landscape can be helped by moving species when they are in trouble, providing corridors along which those that can may move, and intervening to maintain diversity of species in key ecosystems.

Marine and Coastal Environments

Concern about coastal swamps and marshlands comes from their special ecological value and the fact that they are already under stress from human development and pollution. Wetlands have persisted in the past despite slowly changing sea levels. Greenhouse warming could induce sea level rise, however, faster than new wetlands could form. In addition, human activity could constrain such movement if wetlands are bounded by dikes, bulkheads, or other structures. Climate change also could alter upwelling of deep ocean waters or paths of major currents and thus wind and precipitation patterns. Areas of upwelling are among the biologically most productive ocean habitats, and such changes could affect fisheries substantially. We do not understand these phenomena well enough, however, to predict the ecological consequences of coastal or ocean changes with confidence. At present, the potential for human intervention to ease adaptation in marine ecosystems seems limited.

Water Resources

Climate change affects natural seasonal and yearly variations in water resources by changing precipitation, evaporation, and runoff. The first indications that the demand for water is exceeding the supply usually come during drought. Changes in water supply due to greenhouse warming could be moderated, for example, by storage (in natural aquifers or constructed reservoirs) or joint operation of water systems. Demand for water can be reduced through a variety of management techniques, including conservation and price incentives. Constructing dams, canals, and other facilities takes time, and so such adaptation actions need to be taken well in advance. Actions to deal with current variability of water supply should help prepare for the possible consequences of greenhouse warming.

Industry and Energy

Most industrial sectors, including electric power generation, are only moderately sensitive to climate change. Access to regular water supplies is the largest single problem. In most sectors, the planning horizon and lifetime of investments is shorter than the rates of change we could expect from greenhouse warming. In general, industry in the United States will likely adapt to greenhouse warming without much difficulty.

Tourism and Recreation

Tourism and recreation are more sensitive to climate change than some other sectors because part of the industry is closely associated with nature. This part of tourism and recreation will necessarily migrate as the attractive conditions and areas move. Although specific regions will be adversely or favorably affected, for a country as large as the United States, the overall effect will probably be negligible.

Settlements and Coastal Structures

Direct climatic changes of greatest importance to human settlements are changes in the extremes and seasonal averages of temperature, and in the geographic and seasonal distributions of rainfall. Although these direct climatic changes may be important, the secondary effects of greenhouse warming on the levels of water bodies are much more important. Urban areas will probably choose to protect existing sites rather than move. Adaptations can be encouraged by changing building codes and land use planning. Allowances should be made for climate change when long-lived structures or facilities are constructed or renovated.

Human Health

Humans have successfully adjusted to diverse climates. Human health could be affected by greenhouse warming because people are sensitive to climate directly as well as being susceptible to diseases whose carriers, or "vectors," are sensitive to climate. In the United States, however, the rate of improvements in health due to better technology and its application should greatly exceed the threat to health due to climate change. These improvements would not, of course, result from choices about costs and benefits of responding to greenhouse warming as such. The health consequences may be worse in countries with fewer resources.

Migration

Historical evidence suggests that migration over long distances, such as occurred in the United States during the Dust Bowl period, is not an automatic response to climate change. Migrations typically follow established routes and cover relatively short distances. While economic and other stresses will continue to provide incentives for migrants to move to the United States or other industrialized countries, there is unlikely to be climate-driven migration on a scale that could not be managed, at least in the next two decades. What happens over the course of a decade or two, however, can set the stage for developments over the longer term. Nevertheless, taking steps now to prevent future migration would not be justified given human adaptability to change and uncertainties about which areas would be affected.

Political Tranquility

Concern about political tranquility stems from fear that the occasional disaster of today might become persistent tomorrow and that accumulation of problems may become overwhelming. Countries outside the industrial world may lack the institutions or resources to manage additional environmental crises. Difficulties of organizing coordinated, multilateral responses to problems such as hunger are already evident. Greenhouse warming could aggravate present economic, political, and social problems, swamping national governments and international assistance activities and programs.

SOME IMPORTANT INDICES

The same diversity that illustrates how humanity and nature adjust to environmental conditions shows that global averages are inappropriate as foundations for thinking about impact or adaptation. Because most adaptations are local, their cost cannot be calculated until such factors as future water supply can be predicted in specific regions. Strategic indices of greenhouse warming for agencies to monitor and scientists to predict include the following:

1. Seasonal and yearly variation in regional supplies of water to streams and soils.

2. Variability of ocean currents, particularly those affecting regional habitability and coastal life.

3. Variation in regional sea level and inshore height of waves.
4. Variability of the timing of such 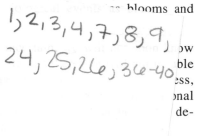 blooms and migrations.

Since even future global averages a low
what these four regional indices will ir ble
to predict local impacts and to desig ess,
monitoring the local climate, includir nal
events, is crucial over time and will de-
signing and selecting these specific a

EVALUATING ADAPTATION OPTIONS

It is difficult to evaluate adaptation options in the face of uncertainties. Consider a hypothetical bridge over an estuary as an example. An added meter of height above sea level might add $100,000 to current construction costs. If that additional clearance were not included at the time of construction, and the sea level rose enough to require it after 50 years, the retrofit raising of the bridge might cost $5 million. Discounted at 6 percent per year, the present value of that $5 million is $271,000. If we were certain the sea would rise, we could realize a benefit of $171,000 in this example by adding the meter of clearance today rather than waiting.

This kind of comparison of current and future investment should be performed when each adaptation option is considered. There are three key elements in this approach: the probability that the outcome will require adaptive action, the discount rate, and the time at which future spending would have to take place. Obviously, reducing our uncertainty about future climate would justify larger investments in adaptations.

Economical adaptation that lessens sensitivity to climate is desirable. Developing drought-resistant crops or using water more efficiently should enable us to deal with weather variability today and position us to cope with future climate change. Poorer countries may have greater difficulties. They typically lack money, information, and expertise. Often they are sorely stressed by current weather extremes, and additional strains accompanying climate change may make their lot worse. If greenhouse warming improves their situation, they may have difficulty taking advantage of their good fortune because of the limits on their capacity to respond.

In general, there are four limits on human responses to greenhouse warming. One is time. Time is needed for people to adapt in a location to a new climate, to design and build new infrastructures, or to adapt by moving to a region where the climate is preferred. Although time is needed to adapt managed things like farming, the historical evidence suggests that farmers can respond, especially in developed countries. The second limit is water. Some uses, like irrigation or cooling, use water in large quantities. Transporting large quantities of water over great distances is possible but expensive. The third limit, and a common one, is money. Adaptations like furnaces and air conditioners, sea walls and canals take money. The fourth limit is techniques and information that are used to make decisions and set priorities.

The recommendations in this report address these areas. It is important that we incorporate these limitations into our thinking when we imagine the effects of the climate of 2030 imposed on the people and landscape of that time.

ADAPTING TO CLIMATE CHANGE

Just as strategic planning requires ranking greenhouse warming with all the other changes ahead, it also demands sorting human activities and nature into classes of sensitivity and adaptability to greenhouse warming alone. Then the more sensitive and serious consequences of greenhouse warming can be ranked within the whole spectrum of changes, and adaptational responses can be decided accordingly. The Adaptation Panel developed the classifications presented in Table 5.1, which are used here to categorize adaptation options with respect to the United States.

Activities with Low Sensitivity

Fortunately, several human activities have low sensitivity, allowing us to concentrate on others. Machinery and buildings are renewed faster than the projected pace of greenhouse warming, and so industry should have little trouble adapting. In general, the decision-making horizons in industry are shorter than the time at which most climatic impacts would emerge. Most industries in countries like the United States can thus be expected to adapt as the climate changes.

The expected climatic changes are within the range people now experience where they live and to which those who move usually learn to adapt. In industrial countries, public health should be less at risk than it is elsewhere. The pace of improvements in health from better technology and public measures can and likely will exceed any deterioration from greenhouse warming. Epidemics from causes already known, failure to control population, and chemical pollution are more serious threats to health than greenhouse warming.

Activities That Are Sensitive But Can Be Adapted at a Cost

As the most valuable outdoor human activity, farming would have the greatest impact on national income due to greenhouse warming. Average warming would not greatly affect yields, but seasonal variations in precipi-

TABLE 5.1 The Sensitivity and Adaptability of Human Activities and Nature

	Low Sensitivity	Sensitive, but Adaptation at Some Cost	Sensitive, Adaptation Problematic
Industry and energy	X		
Health	X		
Farming		X	
Managed forests and grasslands		X	
Water resources		X	
Tourism and recreation		X	
Settlements and coastal structures		X	
Human migration		X	
Political tranquility		X	
Natural landscapes			X
Marine ecosystems			X

NOTE: Sensitivity can be defined as the degree of change in the subject for each "unit" of change in climate. The impact (sensitivity times climate change) will thus be positive or negative depending on the direction of climate change. Many things can change sensitivity, including intentional adaptations and natural and social surprises, and so classifications might shift over time. For the gradual changes assumed in this study, the panel believes these classifications are justified for the United States and similar nations.

SOURCE: Chapter 5 of the report of the Adaptation Panel.

tation and evaporation would. Experience shows, however, that farming must continually adapt to cope with, and even exploit, the stresses and fickle nature of climate. Adaptations to climate change would be required in both rich and poor countries to protect crops, substitute new ones, and protect their foundations of soil and water.

Although less thoroughly managed than farming and growing a crop with a long life, regeneration and management techniques are available that should enable needed forest products to be sustained.

Should climate warm, most cities would try to adapt rather than abandon their sites. Although the adaptation might be costly, the costs would in most cases be lower than the cost of moving the city. By far the highest costs would be in coastal cities, where added protection would be needed in response to storms if the sea rises. Where the coast is thinly settled, protective zoning or even retreat may be sensible.

For the nation as a whole, tourism and recreation seem adaptable to greenhouse warming at little net cost. Adaptation within a country or a region, however, may entail switching a function or activity from one geographical area to another. Some regions may win a new activity, while the same activity becomes untenable and is lost in another. The gradual changes foreseen in this study will combine these pluses and minuses, with a likely small net change for a nation of our size and diversity.

Activities That Are Sensitive with Questionable Adjustment or Adaptation

In the unmanaged systems of plants and animals that occupy much of our landscape and oceans, however, the rate of change of some key processes may be slower than the pace of greenhouse warming, making their future questionable. Unmanaged ecosystems respond relatively slowly, and hence their adaptability to greenhouse warming is more questionable than that of the managed systems of crops on a farm or timber in a plantation.

This slow response comes from the long lives of some of their components, like trees that last longer than the ones planted for timber. It comes from the slow and chancy arrival of seed and birds traveling on the wind, in currents, or along corridors rather than being intentionally transported and planted by farmers. Response is slow because the replacement of plants and animals on an acre of wild land or in an estuary can take decades or centuries and because evolution takes centuries or millennia.

Greenhouse warming would not likely make land barren except at the arid extremes of existing climates if climate became drier. What *is* likely are changes in the composition of ecological communities in favor of those species that are able to move rapidly and far and the disappearance of some species that move slowly. Marine plants and animals inhabiting intertidal regions of rocky shores undoubtedly would be affected by rising sea level. Coral reefs, which are breeding and feeding areas for many of the world's tropical fisheries, could suffer because they appear to be particularly sensitive to water temperature changes.

Although the impacts of the whole range of climatic changes on the functioning of ecosystems cannot be predicted with confidence, the risk of their happening justifies some of the adaptation strategies recommended in Chapter 9 and adds to the justification for some of the mitigation strategies.

Cataclysmic Climatic Changes

Large changes in climate have happened in the past. Desperate masses of people have fled drought or flood in places with marginal farming and growing population. These disasters occurred before greenhouse gases began increasing, and they could occur again. The panel knows of no convincing attempt, however, to compute the probability of cataclysmic changes such as the stopping of the current that warms Europe. Because the probability and nature of such unexpected changes are unknown, the panel cannot project their impacts or devise adaptations to them.

CONCLUSIONS

As discussed in Chapter 3, a rise in global average temperatures in the next century above those of any period in the last 200,000 years cannot be excluded. Unfortunately, there currently is no way to reliably determine the effects of such global changes for particular regions. These changes will probably be gradual. People in the United States likely will have no more difficulty adapting to such future changes than to the most severe conditions in the past, such as the Dust Bowl.*   Other countries may have more

----

*Jessica Mathews, a member of the Synthesis Panel, disagrees with this conclusion with the following statement. "The analysis does not support the conclusion that greenhouse warming will be no more demanding than past climatic changes. If the change is unprecedented in the experience of the human species, how can it be claimed that people will have no more difficulty adapting to future changes than to those of the past?

"The reasoning used here is that human economic activities are largely divorced from nature and that modern technology effectively buffers us from climate. Combined with assumptions of gradual change, no surprises, and an olympian perspective on national costs, the result is an unduly sanguine outlook. Even as a portrayal of a best case scenario (rather than a most likely one), this is a flawed analysis.

"First, it underestimates the extent to which human societies, even affluent ones, depend on the underpinning of natural systems. While recognizing that the pace of greenhouse warming will most likely exceed the rate at which species and ecosystems can adapt, the study does not go on to examine the resulting impacts of severe ecosystem disruption on human societies.

"Also, the impacts of climate change on economic activities are considered separately, sector by sector (farming, industry, transportation, etc). This is understandable given the great difficulty of analyzing the interactions, but here the compartmentalization of impacts in both the natural and economic spheres seems to have led to the distorted view that people, economic activity, infrastructure, and natural context can be disassociated. The finding that 'expected climatic changes are within the range people now experience . . . and to which those who move usually learn to adapt,' means nothing about adaptation to greenhouse-induced change. The fact that one can move with ease from Vermont to Miami has nothing to say about the consequences of Vermont acquiring Miami's climate.

"Reasoning from the experience of past adaptations is risky given that in the past societies could usually expect that climate fifty years hence would be reasonably

difficulty, especially poor countries or those with fewer climate zones. Some natural systems of plants and animals would be stressed beyond sustainability in their current form, a prospect some people may find unacceptable. The stronger the concern about these various changes, the greater the motivation to slow greenhouse warming.

In addition, the panel has not found it possible to rule out or rule in such major disturbances as sudden and major changes in regional climates, ocean currents, atmospheric circulations, or other natural or social phenomena. At present, it is not possible to analyze their likelihood or consequences.

Human societies and natural systems of plants and animals change over time and react to changing climate just as they react to other forces. It would be fruitless to try to maintain all human and natural communities in their current forms. There are actions that can be undertaken now, however, to help people and natural systems adjust to some of the anticipated impacts of greenhouse warming. The panel recommends action now (see Chapter 9) based on gradual climate change. Such action would be more important if climate change proved to be sudden and unanticipated rather than smooth and predictable.

---

like that of the present. This will probably not be the case during a greenhouse warming, because of the difficulties of forecasting regional impacts, the rate of expected change, and because we may be operating under conditions with which mankind has no past experience.

"Finally, it may be strictly accurate that regional 'pluses and minuses' will combine to produce 'small net change for a nation of our size.' But the distribution of impacts in time and space matters more than this treatment suggests. Costs that are indisputably enormous (including human suffering) begin to appear deceptively manageable when viewed solely from the perspective of their impacts on a multitrillion dollar economy. For example, in the case of cities, the study finds that while 'adaptation might be costly, the costs would in most cases be lower than the cost of moving the city.' "

6

Mitigation

Greenhouse warming is a global phenomenon, an important fact with regard to mitigation because releases of greenhouse gases have the same potential effect on global climate regardless of their country of origin. An efficient mitigation strategy for the United States would allow the United States to take cooperative action in other countries; some of the most attractive low-cost mitigation options may be in the poorest developing countries.

This analysis of mitigation costs and the potential for reducing potential greenhouse warming was developed by the Mitigation Panel and is derived almost entirely from experience and data in the United States. The analytical framework is general, however, and could be applied in other countries.

The application of this framework to a diverse array of mitigation options is a pioneering effort. These "first-order" analyses are meant only to be initial estimates of the cost-effectiveness of these options. They demonstrate a method that can be used in determining appropriate mitigation options. The intent is to illustrate the manner in which options should be evaluated with the best estimates available.

This analysis is a cross-sectional, as opposed to a longitudinal, analysis of options over time. It does not attempt, for example, to project future levels of economic activity and their implications for greenhouse gas emissions. The analysis does account, however, for future consequences of current actions. The direct effect of each option on greenhouse gas emissions is assessed. The panel does not examine those options under the different overall emission rates that might occur at future times. This analysis must therefore be seen as an initial assessment of mitigation options in terms of their return on investment under current conditions. A subsequent analysis should consider appropriate strategies under conditions existing at the time.

THE ROLE OF COST-EFFECTIVENESS

A mitigation strategy should use options that minimize effects on domestic or world economies. Strategies therefore should be evaluated on the basis of cost-effectiveness as well as other considerations. Care must be taken to ensure that estimates of both costs and effects are comparable. Cost calculations, for example, need to use consistent assumptions about energy prices, inflation, or discount rates. Benefits must be evaluated in standard terms, such as the equivalent amount of CO_2 emission reductions.

The cost of mitigation may include a number of components, some of which are difficult to measure. Three different kinds of costs need to be distinguished. First are direct expenditures to reduce emissions or otherwise reduce potential greenhouse warming. These include, for example, the purchasing of energy-efficient air conditioners or insulation. Second are long-term investments that increase the overall efficiency of large-scale systems. Examples include investment in more efficient electricity generation and industrial facilities. Third are possible substitutions among final goods and services that require different amounts of energy. An example is the substitution of public transit for private automobiles.

Current expenditures to reduce greenhouse warming are in principle the easiest to measure because there generally are current market transactions from which to obtain data. For longer-term capital expenditures, a discount rate must be used to calculate the present value of costs so they can be compared with costs of other options. Where major substitutions of final goods or services are required, the full costs are difficult to determine. The potential loss in value to consumers of the changes in consumption patterns must be estimated.

TECHNOLOGICAL COSTING VERSUS ENERGY MODELING

There are two choices for estimating the costs of various mitigation options: "technological costing" and "energy modeling." Technological costing develops estimates on the basis of a variety of assumptions about the technical aspects, together with estimates—often no more than guesses—of the costs of implementing the required technology. This approach can be useful for evaluating emerging technologies when it is hard to apply statistical methods to estimate costs from market data. Technological costing relies implicitly on economic assumptions, and like energy modeling assumes that direct costs are a good measure of total cost.

Energy modeling uses a variety of techniques to project energy uses and supplies by region over time. Often, energy modeling uses data on prices and quantities consumed to construct statistical behavioral relationships. Unlike technological costing, energy models strive to ensure that the projections are internally consistent by keeping track of the overall relationship between energy supplies and demands.

Neither approach is perfect. Technological costing studies are often criticized as providing overly optimistic estimates. Their main weaknesses are that they are not always consistent with observed market behavior and that they sometimes fail to allow for impacts on quantities and prices in other markets and therefore neglect "general equilibrium" effects of major actions undertaken. Energy modeling analyses are challenged because of weaknesses in model specification, measurement error, and questionable relevance of historical data and behavior for future untested policy actions.

In this study, the cost-effectiveness indicators for mitigation actions are derived mostly from technological costing rather than energy modeling analyses. In some instances, these analyses show mitigation actions yielding a net savings, implying that investment in these actions would yield a positive economic return. Realizing such net savings, however, would require a set of conditions not now in existence. In other words, achieving such savings would require overcoming private or public barriers of various kinds. If these impediments can be overcome at relatively low cost, society could achieve substantial benefits from these actions, often even if greenhouse warming were not a problem.

Technological costing and energy modeling are in rough agreement, given the large uncertainties in the best available knowledge. This enhances the credibility of the results.

PLANNING A COST-EFFECTIVE POLICY

Investment involves choosing among alternative uses of resources. Finding the least-cost mix of responses to greenhouse warming entails comparing all the different possible responses. Figure 6.1 illustrates that the least-cost plan will probably involve a mix of responses. For simplicity, only two hypothetical options are plotted. They are shown as curves giving the cost for achieving various reductions in greenhouse gas emissions (or the equivalent: removal of greenhouse gases from the atmosphere, blocking of incident radiation, or changing the earth's reflectivity). For comparability, all responses are translated into CO_2-equivalent emissions.

Both options exhibit increasing cost for increasing reductions in emission (the curves gradually bend upward). If the only alternative were to achieve the desired level of reduction by choosing one option, the clear preference would be option B. Option B produces each level of reduction at lower cost (c'') than option A (c').

If, however, it were possible to select some of option A and some of option B, the greatest payoff would come from a mixture of the two. Option B should be selected up to the point at which the cost of additional reductions with option B exceeds the cost of the first reductions with option A (shown by the dashed line). Thereafter, the most cost-effective strategy would be to select some of A and some of B until the desired level of reduction is achieved.

Figure 6.2 extends the comparison to additional options with different characteristics. Option C shows "negative cost," or net positive benefits, associated with achieving the initial reductions in CO_2 emissions. An example is energy conservation, such as better insulating of hot water heaters to reduce heat loss. The cost of insulating would be less than the cost of adding electricity generating capacity if the conservation measures were not implemented.

Option D illustrates a "backstop technology." A backstop technology provides an unlimited amount of reduction at a fixed cost. An example would be an abundant energy source that provides electricity with no CO_2 emissions at all. Where a backstop technology exists, its cost sets a ceiling on the investment in reducing emissions. Only options costing less than D should be considered, no matter how much emission reduction is desired.

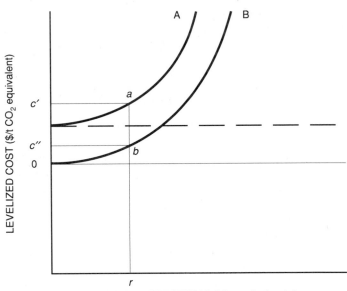

FIGURE 6.1 A comparison of hypothetical mitigation options. Curves show the costs of various levels of reduction in CO_2-equivalent emissions. Total costs for the period of the analysis are divided by the number of years, and all comparisons over time are assumed to be on the same basis.

SOURCE: Chapter 2 of the report of the Mitigation Panel.

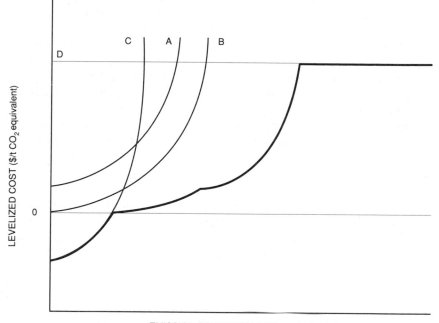

FIGURE 6.2 A comparison of multiple mitigation options. Curves show the costs of various levels of reduction in CO_2-equivalent emissions for four hypothetical mitigation options. Total costs for the period of analysis are divided by the number of years, and all comparisons over time are assumed to be on the same basis.

SOURCE: Chapter 2 of the report of the Mitigation Panel.

The heavy line in Figure 6.2 shows the cost-effective combination of options. Option C is selected up to the point at which option B becomes more cost-effective. Option A is added when it becomes cost-effective. The heavy line showing the cost-effective combination becomes horizontal when the cost reaches that of the backstop technology.

AN ASSESSMENT OF MITIGATION OPTIONS IN THE UNITED STATES

Several premises are central to the design of a well-conceived mitigation policy. First, responses to greenhouse warming should be regarded as investments in the future of the nation and the planet. The actions required will have to be implemented over a long period of time. They must, however, be compared to other claims on the nation's resources.

Second, cost-effectiveness is an essential guideline. The changes in energy, industrial practices, land use, agriculture, and forestry that are likely to be needed to limit emissions of greenhouse gases require investments over time. These are likely to be large enough to affect the economy in various ways. The sensible guideline is cost-effectiveness: obtaining the largest reduction in greenhouse gas emissions at the lowest cost.

A true cost-effectiveness analysis of reducing greenhouse gas emissions would measure only the costs of interventions taken solely because of greenhouse warming. This is difficult in practice because many of these actions contribute to several social goals, making it hard to distinguish the costs and benefits attributable to greenhouse warming alone. There are two ways such complications might be handled: by adding benefits to reflect contributions to multiple goals or by reducing costs to reflect their allocation among different goals. For example, eliminating CFC emissions would slow both the depletion of the ozone layer and the onset of greenhouse warming. A proper accounting of reducing CFC emissions would either assign additional benefits to reflect those gained in the area of ozone depletion or reduce the cost allocated to greenhouse warming proportionate to the contribution of those actions to other goals. In either case, the cost-effectiveness ratio would be improved if multiple social goals were considered. Similarly, several actions that would reduce greenhouse gas emissions are mandated by the Clean Air Act. A full cost-effectiveness analysis would account for the fact that society has already decided to bear these costs, so that only additional costs and benefits would be included in the analysis of greenhouse warming. Limits on time and resources precluded complete analysis of these complications in this study, and the results presented here should be considered a first cut that points the way for further analyses.

Third, a mixed strategy is essential. A least-cost approach produces a variety of options. A mixed strategy, however, requires comparison of options in different sectors of the economy.

In comparing various mitigation options, this panel emphasizes three factors. The first factor is the cost-effectiveness of the option. In calculating cost-effectiveness, the panel converted reductions of all greenhouse gases into CO_2-equivalent emission reduction in order to be able to compare all options on the same basis.

The second factor is the ease or difficulty of implementation of the option. Although a particular option may be technically possible for relatively wealthy countries, it may be precluded for social, economic, or political reasons. These implementation obstacles are different for each option considered. The panel estimates emission reductions that could be achieved if explicitly defined feasible opportunities were executed. For example, one option calls for reducing energy use in residential lighting by 50 percent through replacement of incandescent lighting (2.5 interior light bulbs and 1 exterior light bulb per residence) with compact fluorescent lights. Another option calls for improving on-road fuel economy to 25 miles per gallon (32.5 mpg in Corporate Average Fuel Economy (CAFE) terms) in light vehicles by implementing existing technologies that would not require changes in size or attributes of vehicles. Each option is also evaluated in terms of an optimistic "upper-bound" (100 percent achievement) or a pessimistic "lower-bound" (25 percent) level of implementation. A brief description of the mitigation options considered in this study is found in Table 6.1.

The third factor is the interconnectedness of the option to other issues in addition to greenhouse warming, for example, destruction of the ozone layer or biological extinction. These additional factors, however, were considered only in a qualitative manner and are part of the reason that recommendations are not based solely on the cost-effectiveness calculations developed in this study.

Table 6.2 shows selected mitigation options in order of cost-effectiveness. Some options, primarily in energy efficiency and conservation, have substantial potential to mitigate greenhouse warming with net savings or very low net cost. However, they have not been fully adopted because of various implementation obstacles.

Net savings does not mean that no expenditure is required to implement these options. Rather, it indicates that the total discounted cost of the option over the period of analysis is less than its discounted direct benefit, usually reduction in energy consumption, where the discount rate is 6 percent. At higher discount rates the relative cost would rise. These are options that ought to be, and probably will be, implemented, since they are in the interests of those who implement them. The decisions to start, however, can be hastened through better information and incentives.

Table 6.2 also includes some options that are more costly, face substantial obstacles to their implementation, or have other costs or benefits that are difficult to characterize. For example, reduction of CFC consumption is also beneficial in reducing stratospheric ozone depletion, and the combined benefit derived for greenhouse warming and ozone depletion would raise CFC control options in the ranking of preferred actions. Questions about the appropriateness of current technologies and public opposition to nuclear power, however, currently make this option difficult to implement. To the extent that concern about greenhouse warming replaces concern about nuclear energy and "inherently safe" nuclear plants are developed, this option increases its priority ranking.

Table 6.3 presents what the panel calls geoengineering options. The geoengineering options in this preliminary analysis include several ways of reducing temperature increases by screening sunlight (e.g., space mirrors, stratospheric dust, multiple balloons, stratospheric soot, and stimulating cloud condensation nuclei) as well as stimulation of ocean uptake of CO_2. Several

TABLE 6.1 Brief Descriptions of Mitigation Options Considered in This Study for the United States

---

RESIDENTIAL AND COMMERCIAL ENERGY MANAGEMENT

Electricity Efficiency Measures

White Surfaces/Vegetation	Reduce air conditioning use and the urban heat island effect by 25% through planting vegetation and painting roofs white at 50% of U.S. residences.
Residential Lighting	Reduce lighting energy consumption by 50% in all U.S. residences through replacement of incandescent lighting (2.5 inside and 1 outside light bulb per residence) with compact fluorescents.
Residential Water Heating	Improve efficiency by 40 to 70% through efficient tanks, increased insulation, low-flow devices, and alternative water heating systems.
Commercial Water Heating	Improve efficiency by 40 to 60% through residential measures mentioned above, heat pumps, and heat recovery systems.
Commercial Lighting	Reduce lighting energy consumption by 30 to 60% by replacing 100% of commercial light fixtures with compact fluorescent lighting, reflectors, occupancy sensors, and daylighting.
Commercial Cooking	Use additional insulation, seals, improved heating elements, reflective pans, and other measures to increase efficiency 20 to 30%.
Commercial Cooling	Use improved heat pumps, chillers, window treatments, and other measures to reduce commercial cooling energy use by 30 to 70%.
Commercial Refrigeration	Improve efficiency 20 to 40% through improved compressors, air barriers and food case enclosures, and other measures.
Residential Appliances	Improve efficiency of refrigeration and dishwashers by 10 to 30% through implementation of new appliance standards for refrigeration, and use of no-heat drying cycles in dishwashers.
Residential Space Heating	Reduce energy consumption by 40 to 60% through improved and increased insulation, window glazing, and weather stripping along with increased use of heat pumps and solar heating.
Commercial and Industrial Space Heating	Reduce energy consumption by 20 to 30% using measures similar to that for the residential sector.
Commercial Ventilation	Improve efficiency 30 to 50% through improved distribution systems, energy-efficient motors, and various other measures.

TABLE 6.1 *(continued)*

Oil and Gas Efficiency	Reduce residential and commercial building fossil fuel energy use by 50% through improved efficiency measures similar to the ones listed under electricity efficiency.
Fuel Switching	Improve overall efficiency by 60 to 70% through switching 10% of building electricity use from electric resistance heat to natural gas heating.

INDUSTRIAL ENERGY MANAGEMENT

Co-generation	Replace existing industrial energy systems with an additional 25,000 MW of co-generation plants to produce heat and power simultaneously.
Electricity Efficiency	Improve electricity efficiency up to 30% through use of more efficient motors, electrical drive systems, lighting, and industrial process modifications.
Fuel Efficiency	Reduce fuel consumption up to 30% by improving energy management, waste heat recovery, boiler modifications, and other industrial process enhancements.
Fuel Switching	Switch 0.6 quads[a] of current coal consumption in industrial plants to natural gas or oil.
New Process Technology	Increase recycling and reduce energy consumption primarily in the primary metals, pulp and paper, chemicals, and petroleum refining industries through new, less energy intensive process innovations.

TRANSPORTATION ENERGY MANAGEMENT

Vehicle Efficiency

Light Vehicles	Use technology to improve on-road fuel economy to 25 mpg (32.5 mpg in CAFE[b] terms) with no changes in the existing fleet.
	Improve on-road fuel economy to 36 mpg (46.8 mpg CAFE) with measures that require changes in the existing fleet such as downsizing.
Heavy Trucks	Use measures similar to that for light vehicles to improve heavy truck efficiency up to 14 mpg (18.2 mpg CAFE).
Aircraft	Implement improved fanjet and other technologies to improve fuel efficiency by 20% to 130 to 140 seat-miles per gallon.

(Table 6.1 continues)

TABLE 6.1 *(continued)*

Alternative Fuels

Methanol from Biomass	Replace all existing gasoline vehicles with those that use methanol produced from biomass.
Hydrogen from Nonfossil Fuels	Replace gasoline with hydrogen created from electricity generated from nonfossil fuel sources.
Electricity from Nonfossil Fuels	Use electricity from nonfossil fuel sources such as nuclear and solar energy directly in transportation vehicles.
Transportation Demand Management	Reduce solo commuting by eliminating 25 per cent of the employer-provided parking spaces and placing a tax on the remaining spaces to reduce solo commuting by an additional 15 percent.

ELECTRICITY AND FUEL SUPPLY

Heat Rate Improvements	Improve heat rates (efficiency) of existing plants by up to 4% through improved plant operation and maintenance.
Advanced Coal	Improve overall thermal efficiency of coal plants by 10% through use of integrated gasification combined cycle, pressurized fluidized-bed, and advanced pulverized coal combustion systems.
Natural Gas	Replace all existing fossil-fuel-fired plants with gas turbine combined cycle systems to both improve thermal efficiency of current natural gas combustion systems and replace fossil fuels such as coal and oil that generate more CO_2 than natural gas.
Nuclear	Replace all existing fossil-fuel-fired plants with nuclear power plants such as advanced light-water reactors.
Hydroelectric	Replace fossil-fuel-fired plants with remaining hydroelectric generation capability of 2 quads.
Geothermal	Replace fossil-fuel-fired plants with remaining geothermal generation potential of 3.5 quads.
Biomass	Replace fossil-fuel-fired plants with biomass generation potential of 2.4 quads.
Solar Photovoltaics	Replace fossil-fuel-fired plants with solar photovoltaics generation potential of 2.5 quads.
Solar Thermal	Replace fossil-fuel-fired plants with solar thermal generation potential of 2.6 quads.

TABLE 6.1 *(continued)*

Wind	Replace fossil-fuel-fired plants with wind generation potential of 5.3 quads.
CO_2 Disposal	Collect and dispose of all CO_2 generated by fossil-fuel-fired plants into the deep ocean or depleted gas and oil fields.

NONENERGY EMISSION REDUCTION

Halocarbons

Not-in-kind	Modify or replace existing equipment to use non-CFC materials as cleaning and blowing agents, aerosols, and refrigerants.
Conservation	Upgrade equipment and retrain personnel to improve conservation and recycling of CFC materials.
HCFC/HFC-Aerosols, etc.	Substitute cleaning and blowing agents and aerosols with fluorocarbon substitutes.
HFC-Chillers	Retrofit or replace existing chillers to use fluorocarbon substitutes.
HFC-Auto Air Conditioning	Replace existing automobile air conditioners with equipment that utilizes fluorocarbon substitutes.
HFC-Appliance	Replace all domestic refrigerators with those using fluorocarbon substitutes.
HCFC-Other Refrigeration	Replace commercial refrigeration equipment such as that used in supermarkets and transportation with that using fluorocarbon substitutes.
HCFC/HFC-Appliance Insulation	Replace domestic refrigerator insulation with fluorocarbon substitutes.

Agriculture (domestic)

Paddy Rice	Eliminate all paddy rice production.
Ruminant Animals	Reduce ruminant animal production by 25%.
Nitrogenous Fertilizers	Reduce nitrogenous fertilizer use by 5%.
Landfill Gas Collection	Reduce landfill gas generation by 60 to 65% by collecting and burning in a flare or energy recovery system.

GEOENGINEERING

Reforestation	Reforest 28.7 Mha of economically or environmentally marginal crop and pasture lands and nonfederal forest lands to sequester 10% of U.S. CO_2 emissions.

(Table 6.1 continues)

TABLE 6.1 *(continued)*

Sunlight Screening

Space Mirrors	Place 50,000 100-km^2 mirrors in the earth's orbit to reflect incoming sunlight.
Stratospheric Dust[c]	Use guns or balloons to maintain a dust cloud in the stratosphere to increase the sunlight reflection.
Stratospheric Bubbles	Place billions of aluminized, hydrogen-filled balloons in the stratosphere to provide a reflective screen.
Low Stratospheric Dust[c]	Use aircraft to maintain a cloud of dust in the low stratosphere to reflect sunlight.
Low Stratospheric Soot[c]	Decrease efficiency of burning in engines of aircraft flying in the low stratosphere to maintain a thin cloud of soot to intercept sunlight.
Cloud Stimulation[c]	Burn sulfur in ships or power plants to form sulfate aerosol in order to stimulate additional low marine clouds to reflect sunlight.
Ocean Biomass Stimulation	Place iron in the oceans to stimulate generation of CO_2-absorbing phytoplankton.
Atmospheric CFC Removal	Use lasers to break up CFCs in the atmosphere.

[a]1 quad = 1 quadrillion Btu = 10^{15} Btu.

[b]Corporate average fuel economy.

[c]These options cause or alter chemical reactions in the atmosphere and should not be implemented without careful assessment of their direct and indirect consequences.

SOURCE: Chapter 11 of the Mitigation Panel report.

options, including space mirrors and removal of CFCs from the atmosphere, are not included among those recommended for further investigation in Chapter 9.

Geoengineering options appear technically feasible in terms of cooling effects and costs on the basis of currently available preliminary information. But considerably more study and research will be necessary to evaluate their potential side-effects, including the chemical reactions that particles introduced into the atmosphere might cause or alter. The data presented in Table 6.3 were developed during the course of the study and represent initial estimates. These or other options may, with additional investigation, research, and development, provide the ability to change atmospheric concentrations of greenhouse gases or the radiative forcing of the planet.

Geoengineering options have the potential to affect greenhouse warming on a substantial scale. However, precisely because they might do so, and because the climate system and its chemistry are poorly understood, these options must be considered extremely carefully. We need to know more about them because measures of this kind may be crucial if greenhouse warming occurs, especially if climate sensitivity turns out to be at the high end of the range considered in this study. Efforts by societies to restrain their greenhouse gas emissions might be politically infeasible on a global scale, or might fail. In this eventuality, other options may be incapable of countering the effects, and geoengineering strategies might be needed. Some of these options are relatively inexpensive to implement, but all have large unknowns concerning possible environmental side-effects. They should not be implemented without careful assessment of their direct and indirect consequences.

TABLE 6.2 Comparison of Selected Mitigation Options in the United States

Mitigation Option	Net Implementation Cost[a]	Potential Emission[b] Reduction (t CO_2 equivalent per year)
Building energy efficiency	Net benefit	900 million[c]
Vehicle efficiency (no fleet change)	Net benefit	300 million
Industrial energy management	Net benefit to low cost	500 million
Transportation system management	Net benefit to low cost	50 million
Power plant heat rate improvements	Net benefit to low cost	50 million
Landfill gas collection	Low cost	200 million
Halocarbon-CFC usage reduction	Low cost	1400 million
Agriculture	Low cost	200 million
Reforestation	Low to moderate cost[d]	200 million
Electricity supply	Low to moderate cost[d]	1000 million[e]

[a]Net benefit = cost less than or equal to zero
   Low cost = cost between $1 and $9 per ton of CO_2 equivalent
   Moderate cost = cost between $10 and $99 per ton of CO_2 equivalent
   High cost = cost of $100 or more per ton of CO_2 equivalent
[b]This "maximum feasible" potential emission reduction assumes 100 percent implementation of each option in reasonable applications and is an optimistic "upper bound" on emission reductions.
[c]This depends on the actual implementation level and is controversial. This represents a middle value of possible rates.
[d]Some portions do fall in low cost, but it is not possible to determine the amount of reductions obtainable at that cost.
[e]The potential emission reduction for electricity supply options is actually 1700 Mt CO_2 equivalent per year, but 1000 Mt is shown here to remove the double-counting effect (see p. 61 for an explanation of double-counting).

NOTE: Here and throughout this report, tons are metric.

SOURCE: Chapter 11 of the Mitigation Panel report.

TABLE 6.3 Cost-Effectiveness Ordering of Geoengineering Mitigation Options

Mitigation Option	Net Implementation Cost	Potential Emission Mitigation (t CO_2 equivalent per year)
Low stratospheric soot	Low	8 billion to 25 billion
Low stratospheric dust, aircraft delivery	Low	8 billion to 80 billion
Stratospheric dust (guns or balloon lift)	Low	4 trillion or amount desired
Cloud stimulated by provision of cloud condensation nuclei	Low	4 trillion or amount desired
Stimulation of ocean biomass with iron	Low to moderate	7 billion or amount desired
Stratospheric bubbles (multiple balloons)	Low to moderate	4 trillion or amount desired
Space mirrors	Low to moderate	4 trillion or amount desired
Atmospheric CFC removal	Unknown	Unknown

NOTE: The feasibility and possible side-effects of these geoengineering options are poorly understood. Their possible effects on the climate system and its chemistry need considerably more study and research. They should not be implemented without careful assessment of their direct and indirect consequences.

Cost-effectiveness estimates are categorized as either savings (for less than 0), low (0 to \$9/t CO_2 equivalent), moderate (\$10 to \$99/t CO_2 equivalent), or high (>\$100/t CO_2 equivalent). Potential emission savings (which in some cases include not only the annual emissions, but also changes in atmospheric concentrations already in the atmosphere—stock) for the geoengineering options are also shown. These options do not reduce the flow of emissions into the atmosphere but rather alter the amount of warming resulting from those emissions. Mitigation options are placed in order of cost-effectiveness.

The CO_2-equivalent reductions are determined by calculating the equivalent reduction in radiative forcing.

Here and throughout this report, tons are metric.

SOURCE: Chapter 11 of the report of the Mitigation Panel.

COMPARING OPTIONS

Table 6.2 shows estimates of net cost and emission reductions for several options. It must be emphasized that the table presents the panel's estimates of the technical potential for each option. For example, the calculation of cost-effectiveness of high-efficiency light bulbs (one of the building efficiency options) does not consider whether the supply of light bulbs could meet the demand with current production capacities. It does not consider the trade-off between expenditures on light bulbs and on health care, education, or basic shelter for low-income families. Nor does it consider aesthetic issues about different sources of illumination.

Care must be taken in developing such a table because there is some "double-counting" among potential mitigation options. For example, implementation of both the nuclear and the natural gas energy options assumes replacement of the same coal-fired power plants. Thus, simply summing up the emission reductions of all options to give total reduction in emissions would overstate the actual potential. The options presented in Table 6.2 have been selected to eliminate double-counting.

Finally, although there is evidence that efficiency programs can pay, there is no field evidence showing success with programs on the massive scale suggested here. There may be very good reasons why options exhibiting net benefit on the table are not fully implemented today.

Figure 6.3 illustrates the results of different rates of implementation of those options. The many uncertainties in the calculations of both costs and emission reductions have been collapsed into two lines. The line labeled "25% Implementation/High Cost" assumes incomplete implementation of each option (25 percent implementation of feasible opportunities) and the high end of the range of cost estimates for that option (high cost). This line shows a lower bound of what is reasonable to achieve. The line labeled

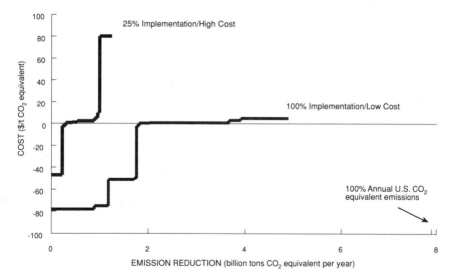

FIGURE 6.3 Comparison of mitigation options. Total potential reduction of CO_2-equivalent emissions is compared to the cost in dollars per ton of CO_2 reduction. Options are ranked from left to right in CO_2 emissions according to cost. Some options show the possibility of reductions of CO_2 emissions at a net savings. See text for explanation.

SOURCE: Chapter 11 of the report of the Mitigation Panel.

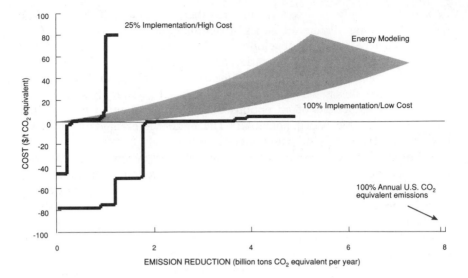

FIGURE 6.4 Comparison of mitigation options using technological costing and energy modeling calculations.

SOURCE: Chapter 11 of the report of the Mitigation Panel.

"100% Implementation/Low Cost" assumes complete implementation of each option (100 percent implementation) combined with the low range of cost estimates for that option (low cost). This line indicates the upper bound that could be achieved with all options shown. A complete analysis would calculate appropriate implementation rates for each option. That is beyond the scope of this study. It should be realistic to achieve emission reduction and cost results somewhere between the two lines in Figure 6.3.

As pointed out earlier in this chapter, technological costing and energy modeling sometimes yield different results. For this reason, both are presented in Figure 6.4. The "100% Implementation/Low Cost" and "25% Implementation/High Cost" curves are repeated from Figure 6.3, and the range typical of energy modeling is shown. As can be seen from Figure 6.4, the United States should be able to achieve substantial reduction in greenhouse gas emissions at low cost, or perhaps even a small net savings.

IMPLEMENTING MITIGATION OPTIONS

An array of policy instruments of two different types are available: regulation and incentives. Regulatory instruments mandate action and include controls on consumption (bans, quotas, required product attributes), production (quotas on products or substances), and factors in design or production (efficiency, durability, processes). Incentive instruments are designed to influence decisions by individuals and organizations and include taxes and subsidies on production factors (carbon tax, fuel tax) and on products and other outputs (emission taxes, product taxes), financial inducements (tax credits, subsidies), and transferable emission rights (tradable emission reductions, tradable credits).

Interventions at all levels could effectively reduce greenhouse warming. For example, individuals could reduce energy consumption, recycle goods, and reduce consumption of deleterious materials. Local governments could control emissions from buildings, transport fleets, waste processing plants, and landfill dumps. State governments could restructure electric utility pricing structures and stimulate a variety of efficiency incentives. National governments could pursue action in most of the policy areas of relevance. International organizations could coordinate programs in various parts of the world, manage transfers of resources and technologies, and facilitate exchange of monitoring and other relevant data.

The choice of policy instrument depends on the objective to be served. Although this analysis of mitigation options does not include all possibilities, the panel is hopeful that it does identify the most promising options. This analysis provides the beginnings of a structure and a process for identifying those strategies that could appropriately mitigate the prospect of greenhouse warming.

CONCLUSIONS

There is a potential to inexpensively reduce or offset greenhouse gas emissions in the United States. In particular, the maximum feasible potential reduction for the options labeled "net benefit" and "low cost" in Table 6.2 totals about 3.6 billion tons (3.6 Gt) of CO_2-equivalent emissions per year. (Here, as elsewhere in the report, tons are metric.) This is a little more than one-third of the total 1990 greenhouse gas emissions in the United States and represents an optimistic upper bound on what could be achieved using these options.

A lower bound can be estimated from Figure 6.4. Arbitrarily using a cutoff of between $10 and $20 per ton of CO_2-equivalent emission reduction would produce a level of about 1 Gt of CO_2-equivalent emissions per year, or a little more than 10 percent of current greenhouse gas emissions in the United States.

This analysis suggests that the United States could reduce its greenhouse gas emissions by between 10 and 40 percent of the 1990 level at very low cost. Some reductions may even be at a net savings if the proper policies are implemented.

7

International Considerations

Effective action to slow greenhouse warming will require international effort regardless of policies in the United States. Many of the cost-effective options appropriate for the United States are also applicable in other countries, including developing nations. The coal resources in China and the Soviet Union alone ensure that without their cooperation, policies aimed at stabilizing greenhouse emissions elsewhere would probably be doomed to failure. Yet the position of the United States as the current largest emitter of greenhouse gases means that action in the rest of the world will be effective only if the United States does its share.

Developing countries may participate in the reduction of greenhouse gas emissions if the first steps are taken by the industrialized countries and if some sort of international agreement is made providing them with additional financial and technical resources to make the necessary changes.

Global population growth, which will largely take place in developing countries, is a fundamental contributor to increasing emissions of greenhouse gases. Developing countries accounted for about 17 percent of world commercial energy consumption 20 years ago, and about 23 percent today. They are expected to account for about 40 percent by 2030. Although it is the industrialized world that contributes most of the current greenhouse gas emissions, this will likely change in the future. Emissions from developing countries will become even more important as they improve their economies and consume more fossil fuels. Either increasing population or growing economic activity can increase emissions of greenhouse gases. Even with rapid technological progress, slowing global population growth is a necessary component for the long-term control of greenhouse gas emissions. Although it may not be financially costly, it is beset with other political, social, and ideological obstacles.

The long-term control of greenhouse gas emissions will require the diffusion and implementation of technology in developing countries. A real challenge will be to ensure that technologies reach those who need them, overcoming such obstacles as lack of information or inability to pay for them. The technological capabilities of developing countries need to be improved. The creation and enhancement of the infrastructure for research and absorption of technology form a precondition for this improvement. Programs in agriculture, forestry, pollution control, and housing might be used both as vehicles for the transfer of relevant technologies and for the enhancement of the research and technology infrastructure.

Similarly, reversing deforestation, to lower atmospheric concentrations of greenhouse gases in the short term, raises a host of issues other than costs. It will be important for international programs to use a broad perspective.

INTERNATIONAL ACTIVITIES

Much work has already been accomplished on the international level, and more is currently under way. Internationally, research on a variety of global change issues (including greenhouse warming) is being undertaken principally under the auspices of two complementary scientific programs: the World Climate Research Program (WCRP) and the International Geosphere-Biosphere Program (IGBP). The WCRP was established by the World Meteorological Organization in 1979 under its overall program, the World Climate Program (WCP). Its major objectives are to determine the extent to which climate can be predicted and the extent of human influence on climate. The IGBP was adopted by the International Council of Scientific Unions (ICSU) in 1986. The objective of the program is to describe the interactive physical, chemical, and biological processes that regulate the total earth system.

In 1988 the World Meteorological Organization and the United Nations Environment Programme sponsored the Intergovernmental Panel on Climate Change (IPCC). At the first IPCC meeting, in November 1988, three working groups were set up: Working Group I, to provide a scientific assessment of climate change; Working Group II, to provide an assessment of the potential impacts of climate change; and Working Group III, to consider response strategies. Hundreds of scientists from different countries contributed to the IPCC report produced in 1990.

The Second World Climate Conference was convened in late 1990 under the sponsorship of several U.N. organizations. The conference was separated into a scientific and technical session and a ministerial session. The conference discussed the results of the first decade of work under the WCP, the First Assessment Report of the IPCC, and the development of the IGBP. The scientific and technical session produced conclusions and recommendations in three areas: (1) greenhouse gases and climate change; (2) use of climate information in assisting sustainable social and economic development; and (3) priorities for enhanced research and observational systems. The ministerial declaration essentially recognized greenhouse warming to be an international problem and urged further elaboration and assessment of response strategies.

A large number of deliberations are under way concerning international negotiations on greenhouse issues. Recent experiences with the Montreal Protocol on Protection of the Ozone Layer and its subsequent elaboration in the London Protocol and with the earlier Law of the Sea provide guidance about what approaches are useful and what to avoid. It is expected, however, that negotiations about limiting greenhouse warming will be more difficult than their predecessors in the environmental area.

FUTURE INTERNATIONAL AGREEMENTS

There is a growing momentum in the international community for completion of an international agreement on climate change in time for signing at the 1992 U.N. World Conference on Environment and Development. The first meeting of the Ad Hoc Working Group of Government Representatives to Prepare for Negotiations on a Framework Convention on Climate Change was held in February 1991. The panel believes that the United States should fully participate in this process.

Identification of priority actions should take full account of their potential to reduce or offset greenhouse gas emissions and their costs of implementation. Further, the panel believes that international arrangements should allow nations to receive credit for actions taken to reduce or offset emissions in other countries. In other words, under such an arrangement countries like the United States could negotiate interventions in other countries if these proved more cost-effective than domestic actions.

OTHER ACTIONS

The importance of multilateral international agreements should not obscure the value of unilateral or bilateral action. The United States should not only adjust its own policies, but also pursue bilateral agreements and technical assistance programs that promote reforestation, protection of biodiversity, and greater energy efficiency.

In framing actions to respond to greenhouse warming, the United States should consider cooperative programs in other countries that might be more cost-effective than domestic options.

8

Findings and Conclusions

This study reviews current knowledge about greenhouse warming and examines a wide variety of potential responses. The panel finds that, even given the considerable uncertainties in our knowledge of the relevant phenomena, greenhouse warming poses a potential threat sufficient to merit prompt responses. People in this country could probably adapt to the likely changes associated with greenhouse warming. The costs, however, could be substantial. Investment in mitigation measures acts as insurance protection against the great uncertainties and the possibility of dramatic surprises. In addition, the panel believes that substantial mitigation can be accomplished at modest cost. In other words, insurance is cheap.

These responses, however, must be based on consideration of the uncertainties, costs of actions and inaction, and other factors. The panel believes they should be based on the approach outlined in Chapter 4. Actions that would help people and natural systems adapt to climate change are described in Chapter 5. Actions to mitigate greenhouse warming are described in Chapter 6.

The findings and conclusions presented here draw on the detailed assessments performed by the other three panels contributing to this study: the Effects Panel, the Mitigation Panel, and the Adaptation Panel. The Synthesis Panel, however, considered additional materials in its deliberations and in the preparation of this report. These include, for example, the reports of the three IPCC working groups, the conference statement from the Second World Climate Conference, statements from other international meetings, publications of the national laboratories and other research organizations in the United States, and documents prepared in other countries. The findings and conclusions of this panel reflect additional analysis, deliberation, and judgment beyond those of the other panels contributing to this study.

POLICY CONSIDERATIONS

The phenomenon of greenhouse warming is complex, and so are the possible responses to it. First, the extent, timing, and variation of future warming and its likely impacts need to be assessed. Second, both the cost and the effectiveness of options to slow greenhouse warming must be estimated and compared to the costs of postponing action. Third, the possible advantages and disadvantages of these actions need to be evaluated in light of the extent to which people, plants, and animals are likely to adjust by themselves or with assistance to changes in the climate. Fourth, the policymaker needs to evaluate these actions in comparison to other ways resources might be used. Before acting, we need to be confident that expenditures to slow climate change make sense. Fifth, decision makers will judge all these factors in a broader context. Responses to greenhouse warming will be determined by people worried about economic growth, food supply, energy availability, national security, and a host of other problems. Many responses appear to produce sizable benefits with regard to other goals, such as reducing air pollution. This study makes no attempt to assess these additional dividends. Instead, it focuses on response to greenhouse warming as such.

Capacities of Industrialized and Developing Countries

Different countries have quite different capacities to respond to change. Poverty, in particular, makes people vulnerable to change and substantially reduces their flexibility in responding to change. Countries with low per-capita income face difficult trade-offs between stimulating economic development and alleviating environmental problems. These countries, which already have difficulty coping with environmental stresses today, will be even more sorely pressed when confronted by climate change.

This report examines response to greenhouse warming in the United States, a country richly endowed with natural and human resources, and one benefiting from a geography that encompasses many climate zones. Compared to many other countries, the United States is well situated to respond to greenhouse warming.

This panel does not attempt to view greenhouse warming from the perspective of a country less well-endowed. Of course, greenhouse warming is a global phenomenon, and many global aspects must be included in any analysis. Nevertheless, most of the data utilized in this study to evaluate mitigation and adaptation options relate to the United States. A more comprehensive examination must wait for future studies.

Taxes and Incentives

Decisions about energy use and other activities that emit greenhouse gases are made daily, even hourly, by 250 million people in the United States in many different areas from transportation to hair drying. Experience here and abroad has shown the inducements of prices and taxes to be a sure way to transmit government policies to decentralized decision makers. Achieving significant reductions in greenhouse gas emissions, however, could involve considerable sacrifice and economic disruption.

There are advantages of market-incentive approaches, but they are not universal. For particular technologies, like the chlorofluorocarbons (CFCs), it may be quicker to use direct regulatory interventions such as emissions limits or caps, although buttressing these with taxes can ensure that the regulations are enforced. An alternative to taxes that has been suggested, and endorsed by several foreign governments and the United States in the Clean Air Act, is establishing emission limits. While this approach seems reasonable on the surface, it has significant shortcomings in implementation.

The major defect with regulatory actions such as emission limits is that there is no easy way that the government can directly control emissions from so many different and separate sources. However, regulation as a technology-forcing mechanism has contributed to reducing emissions of key air pollutants in the United States. It other areas it has been less successful.

Taxes and regulations can discourage or prevent people from taking actions that would increase greenhouse gas emissions; incentives of various kinds can encourage them to act in ways that reduce emissions. If interventions are needed, this panel believes that, in general, incentive-type measures are preferable.

Fundamental and Applied Research

Research is inexpensive in comparison with many other policy options that could make a difference in greenhouse warming. The federal research budget on topics related to global climate change is a little more than $1 billion for fiscal year 1991, which is small in comparison to the expected impact or costs of climate change. Although these funds have been identified as applying to greenhouse warming research, some of them contribute to other objectives as well. Policy should be designed and executed in ways that increase our understanding of the way human activity affects greenhouse warming.

Research on the actual impacts of climate change may identify vulnerabilities and highlight areas for policy action. Every year there are droughts, heat waves, severe storms, and other such phenomena. Understanding how economies and communities of plants and animals are affected by extreme climate events, and whether those responses are changing over time, could provide important guidance for policy choices.

Better understanding of how biological communities function as both sources and sinks of greenhouse gases, especially CO_2, might also help anticipate the consequences of greenhouse warming. More detailed knowledge about phenomena affecting radiative forcing, such as cloud physics and chemistry, or of key mechanisms in the global climate system, such as ocean currents and heat transfers, could help identify where actions might have greatest leverage. Research satellites capable of measuring the energy balance of the earth are necessary, as is maintaining thermometer measurement networks.

Most research up to now has emphasized climatological issues. The global climate change budget in the United States is about 95 percent on the physical phenomena of atmosphere, oceans, and so on and 5 percent on mitigation, adaptation, and impacts. We need to know more about the social and economic processes generating greenhouse gas emissions and about the costs of mitigating these emissions, especially in the energy sector. We need reviews and assessments of policy options to slow climate change, and improvements in the data base for understanding economic and environmental trends relating to global change. Because greenhouse warming is a global problem encompassing a wide range of areas, it will be important to establish programs that are interdisciplinary and examine developing countries as well as high-income countries like the United States.

A PROPOSED FRAMEWORK FOR RESPONDING TO THE THREAT OF GREENHOUSE WARMING

The analyses performed for this study show that the United States should be able to adapt to the changes in climate expected to accompany greenhouse warming. They have also identified a number of options that could slow or offset the buildup of greenhouse gases. Other options could help position us to ease future adaptations to the consequences of greenhouse warming. The fact that people can adapt, or even that they are likely to do so, does not mean that the best policy is to wait for greenhouse warming to occur and let them adapt. Waiting and adapting may sacrifice overall economic improvement in the long run.

The panel has sorted response policies into five categories: (1) reducing or offsetting greenhouse gas emissions, (2) enhancing adaptation to greenhouse warming, (3) improving knowledge for future decisions, (4) evaluating geoengineering options, and (5) exercising international leadership. The recommended options in each category are described in Chapter 9.

GENERAL CONCLUSIONS

In conducting this study, the panel first established the approach and framework described in Chapter 4. The information and data summarized in Chapters 5 and 6 were then gathered and analyzed. On this basis, the Synthesis Panel reached the collective judgment that the United States should undertake not only several actions that satisfy multiple goals but also several whose costs are justified mainly by countering or adapting to greenhouse warming. The panel believes that a systematic implementation of the complete set of low-cost options described in Chapter 9 is appropriate. The panel concludes that options requiring great expenses are not justified at this time.

9

Recommendations

Despite the great uncertainties, greenhouse warming is a potential threat sufficient to justify action now. Some current actions could reduce the speed and magnitude of greenhouse warming; others could prepare people and natural systems of plants and animals for future adjustments to the conditions likely to accompany greenhouse warming.

There are a number of mitigation and adaptation options available to the United States. This panel recommends implementation of the options presented below through a concerted program to start mitigating further buildup of greenhouse gases and to initiate adaptation measures that are judicious and practical. It also recommends a strong scientific program to continue to reduce the many uncertainties. International cooperation is essential in all areas.

The recommendations are generally based on low-cost, currently available technologies. Topics for which new information or techniques must be developed are clearly identified. In many instances, more detailed treatments can be found in the separate reports of the Effects Panel, the Mitigation Panel, or the Adaptation Panel. The numbers in parentheses refer to pages in this report where these topics are discussed.

REDUCING OR OFFSETTING EMISSIONS OF
GREENHOUSE GASES

Three areas dominate the analysis of reducing or offsetting current emissions: (1) eliminating halocarbon emissions, (2) changing energy policy, and (3) utilizing forest offsets. Eliminating CFC emissions is the biggest single contribution in the short run. Energy policy recommendations include reducing emissions related to both consumption and production. Recommendations on both global and domestic programs are included under forest offsets. The United States could reduce or offset its greenhouse gas emissions by between 10 and 40 percent of 1990 levels at low cost, or at some net savings, if proper policies are implemented.

Halocarbon Emissions

Continue the aggressive phaseout of CFC and other halocarbon emissions and the development of substitutes that minimize or eliminate greenhouse gas emissions. (pp. 52, 54-58)

Chlorofluorocarbons not only have a role in the depletion of stratospheric ozone, they also contribute a significant portion of the radiative forcing (i.e., the ability to "trap" heat in the atmosphere) attributable to human activities. The 1987 Montreal Protocol to the Vienna Convention set goals regarding international phaseout of CFC manufacture and emissions. The United States is a party to that agreement as well as to the London Protocol, which requires total phaseout of CFCs, halons, and carbon tetrachloride by 2000 in industrialized countries and by 2010 in developing countries. Unless this agreement is forcefully implemented, the use of CFCs may continue to intensify greenhouse warming. Every effort should be made to develop economical substitutes that do not contribute to greenhouse warming.

Energy Policy

Study in detail the "full social cost pricing" of energy, with a goal of gradually introducing such a system. (pp. 30-31, 67, 68)

On the basis of the principle that the polluter should pay, pricing of energy production and use should reflect the full costs of the associated environmental problems. The concept of full social cost pricing is a goal toward which to strive. Including all social, environmental, and other costs in energy prices would provide consumers and producers with the appropriate information to decide about fuel mix, new investments, and research and development. Such a policy would not be easy to design or implement. Unanticipated winners and losers could emerge, either through improper accounting of externalities, lack of knowledge, or lack of incorporation of other concerns (such as energy security) or through cleverness and innovation. Phasing such a policy in over time is essential to avoid shocks caused by rapid price changes. It would best be coordinated internationally.

Reduce the emission of greenhouse gases during energy use and consumption by enhancing conservation and efficiency (pp. 54-58, 59), including action to:

- Adopt nationwide energy-efficient building codes
- Improve the efficiency of the U.S. automotive fleet through the use of an appropriate combination of regulation and tax incentives
- Strengthen federal and state support of mass transit
- Improve appliance efficiency standards
- Encourage public education and information programs for conservation and recycling
- Reform state public utility regulation to encourage electrical utilities to promote efficiency and conservation
- Sharply increase the emphasis on efficiency and conservation in the federal energy research and development budget
- Utilize federal and state purchases of goods and services to demonstrate best-practice technologies and energy conservation programs

The efficiency of practically every end use of energy can be improved relatively inexpensively. Major reductions could be achieved in energy use in existing buildings through improvements in lighting, water heating, refrigeration, space heating and cooling, and cooking. Gains could be achieved in transportation by improving vehicle efficiency without downsizing or altering convenience. Significant gains could also be achieved in industrial electricity use through fuel switching and improvements in process technologies. Initial calculations show that some options could be implemented at a net savings. There are informational barriers to overcome, however. For example, homeowners may not be aware of the gains to be realized from high-efficiency furnaces. There are also institutional barriers. For example, most public utility commissions disallow a rate of return to power companies on efficiency and conservation options. The panel concludes that energy efficiency and conservation is a rich field for reducing greenhouse gas emissions.

Make greenhouse warming a key factor in planning for our future energy supply mix. The United States should adopt a systems approach that considers the interactions among supply, conversion, end use, and external effects in improving the economics and performance of the overall energy system. (pp. 54-58, 59) Action items include efforts to:

- Develop combined cycle systems that have efficiencies approaching 60 percent for both coal- and natural-gas-fired plants
- Encourage broader use of natural gas by identifying and removing obstacles in the distribution system
- Develop and test operationally a new generation of nuclear reactor technology that is designed to deal with safety, waste management, and public acceptability
- Increase research and development on alternative energy supply technologies (e.g., solar), and design energy systems utilizing them in conjunction with other energy supply technologies to optimize economy and performance

• Accelerate efforts to assess the economic and technical feasibility of CO_2 sequestration from fossil-fuel-based generating plants

The future energy supply mix will change as new energy technologies and greenhouse warming take on increased importance. A "systems approach" should be used to optimize the economics and performance of future energy systems. Interactions among supply options, conversion systems, end use, and external effects should receive much more attention than they have in the past. Actions for improving energy supply systems must cover all important elements in the mix. Also, it is important to prepare for the possibility that greenhouse warming may become far more serious in the future.

Alternative energy technologies are unable currently or in the near future to replace fossil fuels as the major electricity source for this country. If fossil fuels had to be replaced now as the primary source of electricity, nuclear power appears to be the most technically feasible alternative. But nuclear reactor designs capable of meeting fail-safe criteria and satisfying public concerns have not been demonstrated. A new generation of reactor design is needed that adequately addresses the full range of safety, waste management, economic, and other issues confronting nuclear power. Focused research and development work on a variety of alternative energy supply sources could change the priorities for energy supply within the 50-year time span addressed in this study.

Forest Offsets

Reduce global deforestation (pp. 64-65), including action to:

• Participate in international programs to assess the extent of deforestation, especially in tropical regions, and to develop effective action plans to slow or halt deforestation

• Undertake country-by-country programs of technical assistance or other incentives

• Review U.S. policies to remove subsidies and other incentives contributing to deforestation in the United States

In addition to reducing the uptake of CO_2 in plants and soils and being a source of atmospheric CO_2, deforestation contributes to other important problems: loss of species and reduction in the diversity of biologic systems, soil erosion, decreased capacity to retain water in soil and altered runoff of rainfall, and alteration of local weather patterns. The United States now has increasing forest cover, but tropical forests worldwide are being lost at a rapid rate. Nearly every aspect of tropical deforestation, however, is difficult to measure. Even the amount of land deforested each year is subject to disagreement. Nevertheless, action should be initiated now to slow and eventually halt tropical deforestation. Such programs need to be developed by those countries where the affected forests are located in cooperation with other countries and international organizations. Developing countries with extensive tropical forests will require substantial technological and developmental aid if this goal is to be reached.

Explore a moderate domestic reforestation program and support international reforestation efforts. (pp. 54-58, 65-66)

Reforestation offers the potential of offsetting a large amount of CO_2 emissions, but at a cost that increases sharply as the amount of offset increases. These costs include not only those of implementation, but also the loss of other productive uses of the land planted to forests, such as land for food production. Reforesting can, at best, only remove CO_2 from the atmosphere and store it during the lifetime of the trees. When a forest matures, the net uptake of CO_2 stops. If the reforested areas are then harvested, the only true offset of CO_2 buildup is the amount of carbon stored as lumber or other long-lived products. However, the wood might be used as a sustained-yield energy crop to replace fossil fuel use. The acreage available within the United States for reforestation, and the amount of CO_2 that could be captured on these lands with appropriate kinds of trees, are controversial and may be limited. Many details remain to be resolved.

ENHANCING ADAPTATION TO GREENHOUSE WARMING

The nature and magnitude of the weather conditions and events that might accompany greenhouse warming at any particular location in the future are extremely uncertain. This panel examined the sensitivity of the affected human and natural systems to the events and conditions likely to accompany greenhouse warming. The panel's adaptation recommendations are intended to help make the affected systems less vulnerable to future climate change. Most of the recommendations, by making the systems more robust, also help them deal with current climate variability. Some, such as purchasing land or easements for specific habitats or corridors for migration, would not be needed if greenhouse warming does not occur.

Specific adaptation recommendations address agriculture, water systems, long-lived structures, and preservation of biodiversity.

Maintain basic, applied, and experimental agricultural research to help farmers and commerce adapt to climate change and thus ensure ample food. (pp. 36-37)

Farming is the preeminent activity essential to humanity that is exposed to climate. During recent decades, its successful adaptation to diverse climates and changing demand rested on vigorous research and application by both government and business. As climate changes, adapted varieties, species, and husbandry must be more promptly sought and then proven in the reality of fields and commerce. Special challenges are (1) while adapting, to sustain the natural resources of land, water, and genetic diversity that underlie farming; (2) to be productive during extreme weather conditions; (3) to manage irrigation to produce more food with less water; and (4) to exploit the opportunity of increased fertilization provided by more CO_2 in the air.

Make water supply more robust by coping with present variability by increasing efficiency of use through water markets and by better management of present systems of supply. (pp. 38-39)

Currently, weather and precipitation cause natural variability in the water supply, in soil, and in streams, and changes in climate could be expected to produce even greater variability. Fortunately, coping with the present variability makes supply more reliable or robust for future climate change when needed. In many places, supply and demand can be better matched by raising the efficiency of use through changes in rights, markets, and prices, by clever management and engineering of irrigation, and by changes in urban styles of living (e.g., water-efficient landscaping and reduced lawn maintenance). Because the joint management of supplies under the jurisdiction of several agencies can increase water yields substantially, the protracted negotiations for such cooperation should begin now.

Plan margins of safety for long-lived structures to take into consideration possible climate change. (pp. 41-42)

Margins of safety adequate for past climate may be insufficient for a changed climate. Most investments like bridges, levees, or dams have lives as long as the time expected for climate to change. The margins used in constructing such structures are generally computed from the historical frequency of extremes like storms or droughts. The possibility of greenhouse warming must now be considered in computing these margins of safety. A logical procedure for justifying investment in a wider margin of safety now involves two considerations: its cost in terms of its expected present value compared to that of retrofitting the structure when needed, and the probability that the alteration will in fact be needed.

Move to slow present losses in biodiversity (pp. 37-38, 44), including taking action to:

- Establish and manage areas encompassing full ranges of habitats
- Inventory little-known organisms and sites
- Collect key organisms in repositories such as seed banks
- Search for new active compounds in wild plants and animals

- Control and manage wild species to avoid over-exploitation
- Pursue captive breeding and propagation of valuable species that have had their habitats usurped or populations drastically reduced
- Review policies, laws, and administrative procedures that have the effect of promoting species destruction
- Consider purchasing land or easements suitable for helping vulnerable species to migrate to new habitats

Even without greenhouse warming, a series of steps to slow present losses in biodiversity are warranted. Any future climate change is likely to increase the rate of loss of biodiversity while it increases the value of genetic resources. Greenhouse warming therefore adds urgency to programs to preserve our biological heritage. Much remains to be done to ensure that key habitats are protected, that major crop cultivars are collected, and that extensive options are retained for future use. Serious initiatives have only recently been started. In most countries, the driving forces behind the degradation of biodiversity relate to the development context within which people farm; harvest forest products; utilize fresh water, wildlife, and fish; and otherwise invest in land or water. Moreover, there are policies that actually promote destruction by fostering open tillage crops, short-term timber-harvesting concessions, excessive use of water, and inappropriate fishing technology. If climate changes, existing reserves and parks may become unsuitable for species currently living there, and landscape fragmentation may make migration more difficult. Conservation efforts should give more attention to corridors for movement, to assisting species to surmount barriers, and to maintaining species when their natural habitats are threatened.

IMPROVING KNOWLEDGE FOR FUTURE DECISIONS

Data collection and applied research can make exceptional contributions in reducing uncertainties of greenhouse warming. The return on investment in research is likely to be great. The panel identifies the following areas for emphasis: collection and interpretation of data on climate change, improvement in weather forecasting, key physical mechanisms in climate change, and research on the interactions between the biosphere, human activities, and the climate system.

Continue and expand the collection and dissemination of data that provide an uninterrupted record of the evolving climate and of data that are (or will become) needed for the improvement and testing of climate models. (pp. 17-19, 20-23, 24-25)

Current data collection programs should be maintained and should be continued after the new (and different) collection systems (e.g., EOS, the Earth Observing System) have become operational. Earlier modes of collection should be phased out only when the interpretation of new and old data streams has proceeded for an appropriate time. Uncertainties in the climate record and its interpretation should not be exacerbated by change in instrumentation.

Continuous monitoring of key indices that can reveal climate change is needed for identifying adaptations that will be needed in the future. These include the supply of water in the streams and soil of a region, sea level, ocean currents, and dates of seasonal events like blooms and migrations.

Improve weather forecasts, especially of extremes, for weeks and seasons to ease adaptation to climate change. (p. 34)

If storms could be accurately forecast several days in advance, people could prepare for or escape them and hence could live in climates with greater variation and extremes. If extremely cold or dry seasons could be foreseen confidently, appropriate crops could be planted and harvested, and floods and droughts managed more effectively. Continued improvement of several-day forecasts, provision and dissemination of forecasts for additional parts of the world, and increasing knowledge of atmosphere-ocean interactions may help enhance adaptation to greenhouse warming.

Continue to identify those mechanisms that play a significant role in the climatic response to changing concentrations of greenhouse gases. Develop and/or improve quantification of all such mechanisms at a scale appropriate for climate models. (pp. 17-19, 25-26)

Some of the mechanisms already known to need such attention include those involving the role of clouds, the role of the oceans in heat transfer, the possible release of CO_2 in the oceans (i.e., into the atmosphere) with change in ocean temperature, the role of the biosphere in the storage and release of CO_2 and CH_4, and the effect of particle concentrations on cloud cover and radiative balance.

It is also necessary to improve the quantification (at a scale suitable for climate models) of processes such as precipitation, soil moisture, and run-off. Some current mathematical characterizations are unable to provide credible regional projections of these factors even when used for scenarios in which the greenhouse gas concentrations are not changing.

Conduct field research on entire systems of species over many years to learn how CO_2 enrichment alters the mix of species and changes the total production or quality of biomass. Research should be accelerated to determine how greenhouse warming might affect biodiversity. (pp. 37-38, 70)

Communities of plants and animals are complex and intricate. Simplified and controlled experiments in laboratories can help understand them better. Greenhouse warming is likely to increase the rate of loss of biodiversity, and so it adds urgency to experimental programs to preserve our biological heritage. But scientists also must learn how disparate, entire systems of species live and react to changes in their habitats and especially to changes in the concentration of CO_2. The effect of combined CO_2 enrichment and greenhouse warming on the mix of species and other attributes of natural communities cannot be determined without field research conducted over many years.

Strengthen research on social and economic aspects of global change and greenhouse warming. (pp. 69-70)

The U.S. research program has emphasized issues of atmospheric chemistry, climate modeling, and monitoring, while relatively little attention has been given to issues of impacts, mitigation, and adaptation. Major priorities should be (1) improved understanding of the costs for mitigating greenhouse gas emissions, particularly in the energy sector, (2) more detailed studies of the impacts of and adaptations to climate change, (3) a better understanding of the social and economic processes generating greenhouse gas emissions, (4) policy analysis of options and strategies relating to climate change, and (5) improvements in the data base for understanding economic and environmental trends relating to global change.

Greenhouse warming is a global problem; therefore it will be important to encourage interdisciplinary and international programs. Thorough analytical studies of the impacts of greenhouse warming currently are limited to a few relatively high income countries. Yet it is the poor countries, with a large fraction of their population and output in the farm sector, who are the most vulnerable to climate change. In the research areas listed above, it will be important to examine behavior in developing countries as well as in high-income countries like the United States.

EVALUATING GEOENGINEERING OPTIONS

Undertake research and development projects to improve our understanding of both the potential of geoengineering options to offset global warming and their possible side-effects. This is not a recommendation that geoengineering options be undertaken at this time, but rather that we learn more about their likely advantages and disadvantages. (pp. 53-59, 60)

Several geoengineering options appear to have considerable potential for offsetting global warming and are much less expensive than other options being considered. Because these options have the potential to affect the radiative forcing of the planet, because some of them cause or alter a variety of chemical reactions in the atmosphere, and because the climate system is poorly understood, such options must be considered extremely carefully. These options might be needed if greenhouse warming occurs, climate sensitivity is at the high end of the range considered in this report, and other efforts to restrain greenhouse gas emissions fail.

The first set of geoengineering options screens incoming solar radiation with dust or soot in orbit about the earth or in the atmosphere. The second set changes cloud abundance by increasing cloud condensation nuclei through carefully controlled emissions of particulate matter. Despite their theoretical potential, there is convincing evidence that the stratospheric particle options contribute to depletion of the ozone layer. The stratospheric particle options should be pursued only under extreme conditions or if additional research and development removes the concern about these problems. The cloud stimulation option should be examined further and could be pursued if concerns about acid rain could be managed through the choice of materials for cloud condensation nuclei or by careful management of the system. The third class increases ocean absorption of CO_2 through stimulating growth of biological organisms. The panel recommends that research projects be undertaken to improve understanding of both the potential of these options to offset global warming and their possible side-effects. Such assessments should involve international cooperation. This is not a recommendation for implementing these options at this time.

EXERCISING INTERNATIONAL LEADERSHIP

As the largest source of current greenhouse gas emissions, the United States should exercise leadership in addressing responses to greenhouse warming.

Control of population growth has the potential to make a major contribution to raising living standards and to easing environmental problems like greenhouse warming. The United States should resume full participation in international programs to slow population growth and should contribute its share to their financial and other support. (p. 64)

Population size and economic activity both affect greenhouse gas emissions. Even with rapid technological advances, slowing global population growth is a necessary component of a long-term effort to control worldwide emissions of greenhouse gases. Reducing population growth alone, however, may not reduce emissions of greenhouse gases because it may also stimulate growth in per capita income. If the nature of economic activity (especially energy use) changes, some growth will be possible with far less greenhouse gas emissions.

Encouraging voluntary population control programs is of considerable benefit for slowing future emissions of greenhouse gases. In addition, countries vulnerable to the possible impacts of climate change would be better able to adapt to those changes if their populations were smaller and they had higher per-capita income.

The United States should participate fully with officials at an appropriate level in international agreements and in programs to address greenhouse warming, including diplomatic conventions and research and development efforts. (p. 66)

There is a growing momentum in the international community for completion of an international agreement on climate change in time for signing at the 1992 United Nations World Conference on Environment and Development. The United States should participate fully in this activity and continue its active scientific role in related topics. The global character of greenhouse warming provides a special opportunity in the area of research and development. International cooperation in research and development should be encouraged through governmental and private sector agreements. International organizations providing funds for development should be encouraged to evaluate projects meeting demand for energy growth by conservation methods on an equal footing with projects entailing construction of new production capacity.

APPENDIXES

Appendix A

Questions and Answers About Greenhouse Warming

**THE GREENHOUSE EFFECT: WHAT IS KNOWN,
WHAT CAN BE PREDICTED**

1. What is the "greenhouse effect?"

In simplest terms, "greenhouse gases" let sunlight through to the earth's surface while trapping "outbound" radiation. This alters the radiative balance of the earth (see Figure A.1) and results in a warming of the earth's surface. The major greenhouse gases are water vapor, carbon dioxide (CO_2), methane (CH_4), chlorofluorocarbons (CFCs) and hydrogenated chlorofluorocarbons (HCFCs), tropospheric ozone (O_3), and nitrous oxide (N_2O). Without the naturally occurring greenhouse gases (principally water vapor and CO_2), the earth's average temperature would be nearly 35°C (63°F) colder, and the planet would be much less suitable for human life.

2. Why is it called the "greenhouse" effect?

The greenhouse gases in the atmosphere act in much the same way as the glass panels of a greenhouse, which allow sunlight through and trap heat inside.

3. Why have experts become worried about the greenhouse effect now?

Rising atmospheric concentrations of CO_2, CH_4, and CFCs suggest the possibility of additional warming of the global climate. The panel refers to warming due to increased atmospheric concentrations of greenhouse gases as "greenhouse warming." Measurements of atmospheric CO_2 show that the 1990 concentration of 353 parts per million by volume (ppmv) is about one-quarter larger than the concentration before the Industrial Revolution (prior

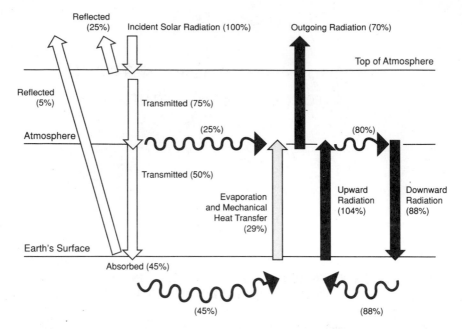

FIGURE A.1 Earth's radiation balance. The solar radiation is set at 100 percent; all other values are in relation to it. About 25 percent of incident solar radiation is reflected back into space by the atmosphere, about 25 percent is absorbed by gases in the atmosphere, and about 5 percent is reflected into space from the earth's surface, leaving 45 percent to be absorbed by the oceans, land, and biotic material (white arrows).

Evaporation and mechanical heat transfer inject energy into the atmosphere equal to about 29 percent of incident radiation (grey arrow). Radiative energy emissions from the earth's surface and from the atmosphere (straight black arrows) are determined by the temperatures of the earth's surface and the atmosphere, respectively. Upward energy radiation from the earth's surface is about 104 percent of incident solar radiation. Atmospheric gases absorb part (25 percent) of the solar radiation penetrating the top of the atmosphere and all of the mechanical heat transferred from the earth's surface and the outbound radiation from the earth's surface. The downward radiation from the atmosphere is about 88 percent and outgoing radiation about 70 percent of incident solar radiation.

Note that the amounts of outgoing and incoming radiation balance at the top of the atmosphere, at 100 percent of incoming solar radiation (which is balanced by 5 percent reflected from the surface, 25 percent reflected from the top of the atmosphere, and 70 percent outgoing radiation), and at the earth's surface, at 133 percent (45 percent absorbed solar radiation plus 88 percent downward radiation from the atmosphere balanced by 29 percent evaporation and mechanical heat transfer and 104 percent upward radiation). Energy transfers into and away from the atmosphere also balance, at the atmosphere line, at 208 percent of incident solar radiation (75 percent transmitted solar radiation plus 29 percent mechanical transfer from the

to 1750). Atmospheric CO_2 is increasing at about 0.5 percent per year. The concentration of CH_4 is about 1.72 ppmv, or slightly more than twice that before 1750. It is rising at a rate of 0.9 percent per year. CFCs do not occur naturally, and so they were not found in the atmosphere until production began a few decades ago. Continued increases in atmospheric concentrations of greenhouse gases would affect the earth's radiative balance and could cause a large amount of additional greenhouse warming. Increasing the capture of energy in this fashion is also called "radiative forcing." Other factors, such as variation in incoming solar radiation, could be involved.

4. Has there been greenhouse warming in the recent past?

Best estimates are that the average global temperature rose between 0.3° and 0.6°C over about the last 100 years. However, it is not possible to say with a high degree of confidence whether this is due to increased atmospheric concentrations of greenhouse gases or to other natural or human causes. The temperature record much before 1900 is not reliable for estimates of changes smaller than 1°C (1.8°F).

5. What about CO_2 and temperature in the prehistoric past?

According to best estimates based on analysis of air bubbles trapped in ice sheets, ocean and lake sediments, and other records from the geologic past, there have been three especially "warm" periods in the last 4 million years. The Holocene optimum occurred from 6,000 to 5,000 years ago. During that period, atmospheric concentrations of CO_2 were about 270 to 280 ppmv, and average air temperatures about 1°C (1.8°F) warmer than modern times. The Eemian interglacial period happened with its midpoint about 125,000 years ago. Atmospheric concentrations of CO_2 were 280 to 300 ppmv, and temperatures up to 2°C (3.6°F) warmer than now. The Pliocene climate optimum occurred between 4.3 and 3.3 million years ago. Atmospheric concentrations of CO_2 have been estimated for that period to be about 450 ppmv, with temperatures 3° to 4°C (5.4° to 7.2°F) warmer than modern times. The prehistoric temperature estimates are from evidence dependent

---

surface plus 104 percent upward radiation balanced by 50 percent of incoming solar continuing to the earth's surface, 70 percent outgoing radiation, and 88 percent downward radiation). These different energy transfers are due to the heat-trapping effects of the greenhouse gases in the atmosphere, the reemission of energy absorbed by these gases, and the cycling of energy through the various components in the diagram. The accuracy of the numbers in the diagram is typically ±5.

This diagram pertains to a period during which the climate is steady (or unchanging); that is, there is no net change in heat transfers into earth's surface, no net change in heat transfers into the atmosphere, and no net radiation change into the atmosphere-earth system from beyond the atmosphere.

on conditions during growing seasons and probably are better proxies for summer than winter temperatures. The estimate for the Pliocene period is especially controversial.

6. What natural things affect climate in the long run?

On the geologic time scale, many things affect climate:
- Changes in solar output
- Changes in the earth's orbital path
- Changes in land and ocean distribution (tectonic plate movements and the associated changes in mountain geography, ocean circulation, and sea level)
- Changes in the reflectivity of the earth's surface
- Changes in atmospheric concentrations of trace gases (especially CO_2 and CH_4)
- Changes of a catastrophic nature (such as meteor impacts or extended volcanic eruptions)

7. What is meant by "atmospheric lifetime" and "sinks?"

These concepts can be illustrated by referring to what is called the "carbon cycle." When CO_2 is emitted into the atmosphere, it moves among four main sinks, or pools, of stored carbon: the atmosphere, the oceans, the soil, and the earth's biomass (plants and animals). The movement of CO_2 among these sinks is not well understood. About 45 percent of the total emissions of CO_2 from human activity since preindustrial times is missing in the current accounting of CO_2 in the atmosphere, oceans, soil, and biomass. Three possible sinks for this missing CO_2 have been suggested. First, more CO_2 may have been absorbed into the oceans than was thought. Second, the storage of CO_2 in terrestrial plant life may be greater than estimated. Third, more CO_2 may have been absorbed directly into soil than is thought. However, there is no direct evidence for any of these explanations accounting for all the missing CO_2. CO_2 in the atmosphere is relatively "long-lived" in that it does not easily break down into its constituent parts. CH_4, by contrast, decomposes in the atmosphere in about 10 years. The greenhouse gas with the longest atmospheric lifetime (except for CO_2), CFC-115, has an average atmospheric lifetime of about 400 years. The overall contribution of greenhouse gases to global warming depends on their atmospheric lifetime as well as their ability to trap radiation. Table A.1 shows the relevant characteristics of the principal greenhouse gases.

8. Do all greenhouse gases have the same effect?

Each gas has different radiative properties, atmospheric chemistry, typical atmospheric lifetime, and atmospheric concentration. For example, CFC-12 is roughly 15,800 times more efficient molecule for molecule at trapping heat than CO_2. Because CFC-12 is a large, heavy molecule with many atoms and a

TABLE A.1 Key Greenhouse Gases Influenced by Human Activity

	CO_2	CH_4	CFC-11	CFC-12	N_2O
Preindustrial atmospheric concentration	280 ppmv	0.8 ppmv	0	0	288 ppbv
Current atmospheric concentration (1990)[a]	353 ppmv	1.72 ppmv	280 pptv	484 pptv	310 ppbv
Current rate of annual atmospheric accumulation[b]	1.8 ppmv (0.5%)	0.015 ppmv (0.9%)	9.5 pptv (4%)	17 pptv (4%)	0.8 ppbv (0.25%)
Atmospheric lifetime (years)[c]	(50-200)	10	65	130	150

[a]The 1990 concentrations have been estimated on the basis of an extrapolation of measurements reported for earlier years, assuming that the recent trends remained approximately constant.

[b]Net annual emissions of CO_2 from the biosphere not affected by human activity, such as volcanic emissions, are assumed to be small. Estimates of human-induced emissions from the biosphere are controversial.

[c]For each gas in the table, except CO_2, the "lifetime" is defined as the ratio of the atmospheric concentration to the total rate of removal. This time scale also characterizes the rate of adjustment of the atmospheric concentrations if the emission rates are changed abruptly. CO_2 is a special case because it is merely circulated among various reservoirs (atmosphere, ocean, biota). The "lifetime" of CO_2 given in the table is a rough indication of the time it would take for the CO_2 concentration to adjust to changes in the emissions.

NOTES: Ozone has not been included in the table because of lack of precise data. Here ppmv = parts per million by volume, ppbv = parts per billion by volume, and pptv = parts per trillion by volume.

SOURCE: World Meteorological Organization. 1990. *Climate Change, the IPCC Scientific Assessment*. Cambridge, United Kingdom: Cambridge University Press. Table 1.1. Reprinted by permission of Cambridge University Press.

CO_2 molecule is small and light in comparison, there are fewer molecules of CFC-12 in each ton of CFC-12 emissions than CO_2 molecules in each ton of CO_2 emissions. Each ton of CFC-12 emissions is about 5,750 times more efficient at trapping heat than each ton of CO_2. The comparatively greater amount of CO_2 in the atmosphere, however, means that it accounts for roughly half of the radiative forcing associated with the greenhouse effect.

9. Do greenhouse gases have different effects over time?

Yes. Figure A.2 shows projected changes in radiative forcing for different greenhouse gases between now and 2030. The potential increase for each gas is plotted for different emissions of each gas compared to 1990 emis-

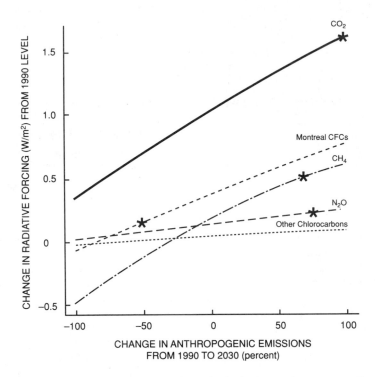

FIGURE A.2 Additional radiative forcing of principal greenhouse gases from 1990 to 2030 for different emission rates. The horizontal axis shows changes in greenhouse gas emissions ranging from completely eliminating emissions (−100 percent) to doubling current emissions (+100 percent). Emission changes are assumed to be linear from 1990 levels to the 2030 level selected. The vertical axis shows the change in radiative forcing in watts per square meter at the earth's surface in 2030. Each asterisk indicates the projected emissions of that gas assuming no additional regulatory policies, based on the Intergovernmental Panel on Climate Change estimates and the original restrictions agreed to under the Montreal Protocol, which limits emissions of CFCs. Chemical interactions among greenhouse gas species are not included.

For CO_2 emissions remaining at 1990 levels through 2030, the resulting change in radiative forcing can be determined in two steps: (1) Find the point on the curve labeled "CO_2" that is vertically above 0 percent change on the bottom scale. (2) The radiative forcing on the surface-troposphere system can be read in watts per square meter by moving horizontally to the left-hand scale, or about 1 W/m^2. These steps must be repeated for each gas. For example, the radiative forcing for continued 1990-level emissions of CH_4 through 2030 would be about 0.2 W/m^2.

SOURCE: Chapter 3 of the report of the Effects Panel.

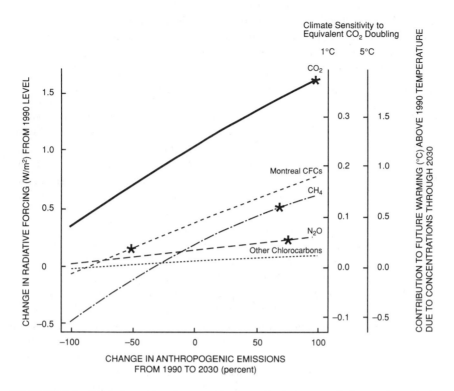

FIGURE A.3 Commitment to future warming. An incremental change in radiative forcing between 1990 and 2030 due to emissions of greenhouse gases implies a change in global average equilibrium temperature (see text). The scales on the right-hand side show two ranges of global average temperature responses. The first corresponds to a climate whose temperature response to an equivalent of doubling of the preindustrial level of CO_2 is 1°C; the second corresponds to a rise of 5°C for an equivalent doubling of CO_2. These scales indicate the equilibrium commitment to future warming caused by emissions from 1990 through 2030. Assumptions are as in Figure A.2.

   To determine equilibrium warming in 2030 due to continued emissions of CO_2 at the 1990 level, find the point on the curve labeled "CO_2" that is vertically above 0 percent change on the bottom scale. The equilibrium warming on the right-hand scales is about 0.23°C (0.4°F) for a climate system with 1° sensitivity and about 1.2°C (2.2°F) for a system with 5° sensitivity. For CH_4 emissions continuing at 1990 levels through 2030, the equilibrium warming would be about 0.04°C (0.07°F) at 1° sensitivity and about 0.25°C (0.5°F) at 5° sensitivity. These steps must be repeated for each gas. Total warming associated with 1990-level emissions of the gases shown until 2030 would be about 0.41°C (0.7°F) at 1° sensitivity and about 2.2°C (4°F) at 5° sensitivity.

   Scenarios of changes in committed future warming accompanying different greenhouse gas emission rates can be constructed by repeating this process for given emission rates and adding up the results.

sion levels. The figure shows the impact of different percentage changes in emissions (compared to 1990 emission rates) on the radiative forcing. Figure A.3 extends this to show the impact on equilibrium temperature for different sensitivities of the climatic system (in degrees Celsius).

10. What is meant by a "feedback" mechanism?

One example of a greenhouse warming feedback mechanism involves water vapor. As air warms, each cubic meter of air can hold more water vapor. Since water vapor is a greenhouse gas, this increased concentration of water vapor further enhances greenhouse warming. In turn, the warmer air can hold more water, and so on. This is an example of a positive feedback, providing a physical mechanism for "multiplying" the original impetus for change beyond its initial force.

Some mechanisms provide a negative feedback, which decreases the initial impetus. For example, increasing the amount of water vapor in the air may lead to forming more clouds. Low-level, white clouds reflect sunlight, thereby preventing sunlight from reaching the earth and warming the surface. Increasing the geographical coverage of low-level clouds would reduce greenhouse warming, whereas increasing the amount of high, convective clouds could enhance greenhouse warming. This is because high, convective clouds absorb energy from below at higher temperatures than they radiate energy into space from their tops, thereby effectively trapping energy. Satellite measurements indicate that clouds currently have a slightly negative effect on current planetary temperature. It is not known whether increased temperatures would lead to more low-level clouds or more high, convective clouds.

11. Can the temperature record be used to show whether or not greenhouse warming is occurring?

The estimated warming of between 0.3° and 0.6°C (0.5° and 1.1°F) over the last 100 years is roughly consistent with increased concentrations of greenhouse gases, but it is also within the bounds of "natural" variability for weather and climate. It cannot be proven to a high degree of confidence that this warming is the result of the increased atmospheric concentrations of greenhouse gases. There may be an underlying increase or decrease in average temperature from other, as yet undetected, causes.

12. What is the basis for predictions of global warming?

General circulation models (GCMs) are the principal tools for projecting climatic changes. GCMs project equilibrium temperature increases between 1.9° and 5.2°C (3.4° and 9.4°F) for greenhouse gas concentrations equivalent to a doubling of the preindustrial level of atmospheric CO_2. The midpoint of this range corresponds to an average global climate warmer than any in the last 1 million years. The consequences of this amount of warming are unknown and may include extremely unpleasant surprises.

13. What is "equilibrium temperature"?

The oceans, covering roughly 70 percent of the earth's surface, absorb heat from the sun and redistribute it to the deep oceans slowly. It will be decades, perhaps centuries, before the oceans and the atmosphere fully redistribute the absorbed energy and the currently "committed" temperature rise is actually "realized." The temperature at which the system would ultimately come to rest given a particular level of greenhouse gas concentrations is called the "equilibrium temperature." Since atmospheric concentrations of greenhouse gases are constantly changing, the temperature measured at any time is the "transient" temperature, which lags behind the committed equilibrium warming. The lag depends in part on the sensitivity of the climate system and is believed to be between 10 and 100 years. This phenomenon makes it difficult to use temperature alone to "prove" that greenhouse warming is occurring.

14. How can we know when greenhouse warming is occurring?

The only tools we have for trying to produce credible scientific results are observations combined with theoretical calculation. Detecting additional greenhouse warming will require careful monitoring of temperature and other variables over years or even decades. Further development of numerical models will help characterize the climatic system, including the atmosphere, oceans, and land-based elements like forests and ice fields. However, only careful interpretation of actual measurements can reveal what has occurred and when.

15. How can credible estimates of future global warming be made?

Several approaches can be used. Scientific "first principles" can be used to estimate physical bounds on future trends. GCMs can be used to conduct "what if" experiments under differing conditions. Comparisons can be made with paleoclimatic data of previous interglacial periods. None of these methods is absolutely conclusive, but it is generally agreed that GCMs are the best available tools for predicting climatic changes. Substantial improvements in GCM capabilities are needed, however, for GCM forecasts to increase their credibility.

16. What influences future warming?

The amount of climatic warming depends on several things:

- The amount of sunlight reaching the earth
- Emission rates of greenhouse gases
- Chemical interactions of greenhouse gases in the atmosphere

- Atmospheric lifetimes of greenhouse gases until they decompose or transfer into sinks
- Effectiveness of positive or negative feedback mechanisms that enhance or reduce warming
- Human actions, which affect radiative forcing in both positive and negative directions

17. What are the major "unknowns" in predictions?

Major uncertainties include:

- Future emissions of greenhouse gases
- Role of the oceans and biosphere in uptake of heat and CO_2
- Amount of CO_2 and carbon in the atmosphere, oceans, biota, and soils
- Effectiveness of sinks for CO_2 and other greenhouse gases, especially CH_4
- Interactions between temperature change and cloud formation and the resulting feedbacks
- Effects of global warming on biological sources of greenhouse gases
- Interactions between changing climate and ice cover and the resulting feedbacks
- Amount and regional distribution of precipitation
- Other factors, like variation in solar radiation

18. How can the uncertainties best be handled?

Data can be arrayed to validate components of the models. Increasing the number of data sets can also help. In addition, the variation in GCM results can be compared to provide a sense of their "robustness." A major "intercomparison" of GCMs is being conducted, and has shown large differences in regional precipitation and reduction of snow and ice fields at high latitudes.

19. Are there changes associated with an equivalent doubling of the preindustrial level of atmospheric CO_2 that can be stated with confidence?

Because of the uncertainty in our understanding of various factors, projections reflect different levels of confidence.

Highly plausible:	Global average surface warming
	Global average precipitation increase
	Reduction in sea ice
	High-latitude surface winter warming
Plausible:	Global sea level rise
	Intensification of summer mid-latitude, mid-continental drying
	High-latitude precipitation increase

Highly uncertain: Local details of climate change
                    Regional distribution of precipitation
                    Regional vegetation changes
                    Increase in tropical storm intensity or frequency

20. What about storms and other extreme weather events?

The factors governing tropical storms are different from those governing mid-latitude storms and need to be considered separately.

One of the conditions for formation of typhoons or hurricanes today is a sea surface temperature of 26°C (79°F) or greater. With higher global average surface temperature, the area of sea with this temperature should be larger. Thus the number of hurricanes could increase. However, air pressure, humidity, and a number of other conditions also govern the creation and propagation of tropical cyclones. The critical temperature for their creation may increase as climate changes these other factors. There is no consistent indication whether tropical storms will increase in number or intensity as climate changes. Nor is there any evidence of change over the past several decades.

Mid-latitude storms are driven by equator-to-pole temperature contrast. In a warmer world, this contrast will probably weaken since surface temperatures in high latitudes are projected to increase more than at the equator (at least in the northern hemisphere). Higher in the atmosphere, however, the temperature contrast strengthens. Increased atmospheric water vapor could also supply extra energy to storm development. We do not currently know which of these factors would be more important and how mid-latitude storms would change in frequency, intensity, or location.

21. Can projections be improved?

Better computers alone will not solve the problems associated with positive and negative feedbacks. Better understanding of atmospheric physics and chemistry and better mathematical descriptions of relevant mechanisms in the models are also needed, as are data to validate models and their subcomponents. Significant improvements may require decades.

22. Is it possible to avoid the projected warming?

It is possible only at great expense or by incurring risks not now understood, unless the earth is itself self-correcting. Continued increases in atmospheric concentrations of greenhouse gases would probably result in additional global warming. Avoiding all future warming either would be very costly (if we significantly reduce atmospheric concentrations of greenhouse gases) or potentially very risky (if we use climate engineering). However, a comprehensive action program could slow or reduce the onset of greenhouse warming.

A FRAMEWORK FOR RESPONDING TO ADDITIONAL GREENHOUSE WARMING

23. What kinds of responses to potential greenhouse warming are possible?

Human interventions in natural and economic activities can affect the net rate of change in the radiative forcing of the earth. It is useful to categorize the possible types of intervention into three types:

- Actions to eliminate or reduce emissions of greenhouse gases
- Actions to "offset" such emissions by removing such gases from the atmosphere, blocking solar radiation, or altering the earth's reflectivity or absorption of energy
- Actions to help human and ecologic systems adjust to new climatic conditions and events

In this study the panel analyzes the first two types of action together under the label of "mitigation," since they are aimed at avoiding or reducing greenhouse warming. The third type of action is here called "adaptation."

24. How can response options be evaluated?

The choice of response options to potential greenhouse warming can be guided by a standard cost-benefit approach, augmented to handle some important aspects of the issues involved. The anticipated impacts (both adverse and beneficial) can be arrayed to produce a "damage function" showing the anticipated costs (or benefits) associated with projected climatic changes. The mitigation and adaptation options can be arrayed similarly according to their respective costs and effectiveness to produce an "abatement cost function." Optimal policies involve balancing incremental costs and benefits, which is called cost-benefit balancing. A necessary condition for an optimal policy is that the level of policy chosen should be cost-effective (any step undertaken minimizes costs). Employing such guidelines requires estimating both the anticipated damages and the cost-effectiveness of alternative response options, and choosing a discount rate to use for assessing the current value of future expenditures or returns.

In practice, a full cost-benefit approach can only be approximated. It is impossible to determine in detail the impacts of climatic changes that will not occur for 40 or 100 years. Thus the damage function can be only roughly approximated. Estimation of the abatement cost function is considerably easier.

Responses to greenhouse warming should be regarded as investments in the future. Cost-effectiveness and cost-benefit balancing should guide the selection of options. In general, a mixed strategy employing some investment in many different alternatives will be most effective.

IMPACTS OF ADDITIONAL GREENHOUSE WARMING

25. Can impacts of expected climatic changes be projected?

It currently is not possible to predict regional temperature, precipitation, and other effects of climate change with much confidence. And without quantitative projections of regional and local climatic changes, it is not possible to produce quantitative projections of the consequences of greenhouse warming.

Instead, the degree of "sensitivity" of affected human and natural systems to the projected changes can be estimated. The sensitivity of a particular system to the climate changes expected to accompany different amounts of additional greenhouse warming can be used to estimate the impacts of those changes.

A crucial aspect of the sensitivity of a system is the speed at which it can react. For example, investment decisions in many industries typically have a "life-cycle" of 10 years or less. Climatic changes associated with additional greenhouse warming are expected to emerge slowly enough that these industries may be expected to adjust as climate changes. Some industries, such as electric power production, have longer investment cycles, and might have more difficulty responding as quickly. Natural ecological systems would not be expected to anticipate climate change and probably would not be able to adapt as quickly as climatic conditions change.

The impacts of climate change are thus hard to assess because the response of human and natural systems to climate change must be included.

26. How can the impacts on affected systems be classified?

Likely impacts of climate change can be divided into four categories:

• Low sensitivity. The projected changes would likely have little effect on the system. An example is most industrial production not requiring large quantities of water. Temperature changes of the magnitude projected would not matter much for most industrial processes. These impacts do not give rise to much concern.

• High sensitivity, but adaptation possible at some cost. The system would likely adapt or otherwise cope with the projected changes without completely restructuring the system. An example is American agriculture. Although some crops would likely move into new locations, agricultural scientists and plant breeders would almost certainly develop new crops suitable for changed growing conditions. There would be costs, but food supply would not be interrupted. As a class, these impacts give rise to concern because the affected systems may have difficulty adapting.

• High sensitivity, and adaptation problematic. The system would be seriously affected, and adaptation would probably not be easy or effective. Natural communities of plants and animals would probably lose their current structure, and reformulate with different mixes of species. Some individual species, especially animals, would move to new locations. The natural landscape as we know it today would almost certainly be altered by a climate change at or above the midpoint of the range used in this study. These impacts are of considerable concern because the affected systems may not be able to adapt without assistance.

• Uncertain sensitivity, but cataclysmic consequences. The sensitivity of the system cannot be assessed with certainty, but the consequences would be extremely severe. An example is the possible shifting, slowing, or even stopping of major ocean currents like the Gulf Stream or the Japanese Current. These ocean currents strongly affect weather patterns, and changes in them could drastically alter weather in Europe or the West Coast of the United States. We have no credible way, however, of assessing the conditions that could lead to such shifts.

27. What are the likely impacts of climate change?

Human societies exhibit a wide range of adaptive mechanisms in the face of changing climatic events and conditions. Projected climatic changes, especially at the upper end of the range, may overwhelm human adaptive mechanisms in areas of marginal productivity and in countries where traditional coping mechanisms have been disrupted. In general, natural ecosystems would be much more sorely stressed, probably beyond their capacities for adjustment. For example, even temperature changes at the lower end of the range would result in shifts of local climates at rates faster than the movement of long-lived trees with large seeds.

A comprehensive catalog of beneficial and harmful impacts is not available. Nor is an estimation of the magnitude of the likely impacts of projected climatic changes. Table A.2 summarizes impacts to human and natural systems in the United States according to the sensitivity categories.

28. Can costs be calculated for the various impacts of projected climate changes?

Not directly. The climatic changes likely to occur in the future cannot be directly measured. The costs and benefits associated with some aspects of certain changes can be estimated, however. These can be used to produce very rough estimates of the costs of climatic impacts. However, these must be recognized as very imprecise indicators.

In general, the costs in the United States associated with the first category of sensitivity are low in relation to overall economic activity. The

TABLE A.2 The Sensitivity and Adaptability of Human Activities and Nature

	Low Sensitivity	Sensitive, but Adaptation at Some Cost	Sensitive, Adaptation Problematic
Industry and energy	X		
Health	X		
Farming		X	
Managed forests and grasslands		X	
Water resources		X	
Tourism and recreation		X	
Settlements and coastal structures		X	
Human migration		X	
Political tranquility		X	
Natural landscapes			X
Marine ecosystems			X

NOTE: Sensitivity can be defined as the degree of change in the subject for each "unit" of change in climate. The impact (sensitivity times climate change) will thus be positive or negative depending on the direction of climate change. Many things can change sensitivity, including intentional adaptations and natural and social surprises, and so classifications might shift over time. For the gradual changes assumed in this study, the panel believes these classifications are justified for the United States and similar nations.

SOURCE: Chapter 5 of the report of the Adaptation Panel.

costs associated with the second category are higher but still should not result in major disruption of the economy. Appropriate adjustments could probably be accomplished without replacing current systems. Costs associated with the third category are much larger, and the adjustments could involve disruption. Some type of anticipation for meeting them may be justified. The category of extremely adverse impacts would be associated with high potential costs and would disrupt most aspects of the system in question. These outcomes, however, are extremely difficult to assess. Table A.3 summarizes some "benchmark" costs illustrative of impacts similar to those that might be associated with climate change.

TABLE A.3 Illustrative Costs of Impacts and Adaptations

Class	Description	Dollars (1990)	Per
GNP	1985 total U.S.	4015 billion[a]	
	1985 average U.S.	17 thousand	capita
	1985 global average	3 thousand	capita
	2100 global average projected	7-36 thousand	capita
	2100 average U.S.[b]	150 thousand	capita
Climate hazards	1980 U.S. heatwave	20 billion	
	1988 U.S. drought	39 billion	
	1983 Utah heavy snow, floods, and landslide	300 million	
	1985 Ohio and Pennsylvania tornados	500 million	
	1985 West Virginia floods	700 million	
	1989 Hurricane Hugo	5 billion	
Recent annual average U.S. losses[c]	Hurricanes	800-1800 million	
	Floods	3 billion	
	Tornados and thunderstorms	300-2000 million	
	Winter storms and snows	3 billion	
	Drought	800-1000 million	
	1988 budget U.S. Weather Service	323 million	
Farming	Create successful wheat variety	1 million	
	Kansas Agricultural Research Experiment Station	33 million	
	U.S. and state agricultural research	2.3 billion	
	1974-1977 drought, federal expenditures[d]	7 billion	
	1986 U.S. farm GNP	76 billion	
Forestry	Prepare and plant	130	acre
	Treat with herbicide	41	acre
	Fertilize	36	acre
	Thin	55	acre
	Protect from fire for 1 year	1.36	acre
	1983 fire protection on state and private forests[e]	245 million	
	1986 U.S. forestry and fishery GNP	17 billion	
Natural landscape[f]	Preserve a large mammal in zoo	1500-3000	year
	Preserve a large bird in zoo	100-1000	year
	Preserve a plant in botanical garden	500	year
	Recover peregrine falcon	3 million	1970-1990
	Recover all endangered birds of prey	5 million	year
	Preserve an acre in a large reserve	50-5000	acre
	1985 expenditure on wildlife-related recreation, including hunting and fishing	55.4 billion	
	Budget National Park Service	1 billion	year

Water[g]	Delaware River above Philadelphia	51	acrefoot
	Sacramento delta	137	acrefoot
	High flow skimming, Hudson River	555	acrefoot
	Desalting	2200-5400	acrefoot
	Present national average	533	acrefoot
	Present irrigation water in California	15	acrefoot
	Annual water bill for domestic use	60	capita
	Annual cost of water for irrigation	45	acre
	Value of an acre of tomatoes	4000	acre
Industry	Raise offshore drilling platform 1 meter[h]	16 million	
	1986 U.S. manufacturing GNP	824 billion	
Settlement[i]	Raise a Dutch dike 1 meter	3 thousand	m length
	Build seawall, Charleston, South Carolina	6 thousand	m length
	Nourish beach for 1 year, Florida	35-200	m length
	Nourish beach for 1 year, Charleston, South Carolina	300	m length
	Hurricane evacuation	35-50	person
	Strengthen coastal property for 100-mph wind	30-90 billion	U.S. coast
	Floodproof by raising house 3 feet	10-40 thousand	house
	Move house from floodplain	20-70 thousand	house
	Levees, berms, and pumps	17 thousand	1/4 acre
	1986 U.S. state and local services	331 billion	
Migration	Resettle a refugee in 1989, federal contribution	7 thousand	person

[a]National Income in 1985 was $3222 billion.

[b]Assumes 1.9 percent growth per year, which is the annual average growth rate for U.S. GNP from 1800 to 1985.

[c]In an extremely adverse year, climate hazards may cost $40 billion or 1 percent of the $4000 billion U.S. GNP, which is about $160 per capita.

[d]During the drought of the 1970s, annual federal expenditures on drought relief averaged about 3 to 4 percent of GNP.

[e]In 1983, expenditures on about a half billion acres of state and private forest land were $0.50 per acre. Increasing expenditures on all forest land to $1.36 per acre would cost about $500 million or 3 percent of forest and fishery GNP.

[f]The cost of recovering all endangered birds of prey is 1 ten-thousandth and the cost of the National Park Service is 2 percent of the annual expenditures on wildlife-associated recreation.

[g]Doubling the cost of domestic water would cost a person a third of a percent of per capita GNP in the United States. Raising the cost of irrigation water from the present $15 per acre-foot to the $137 per acre-foot for the prospective water from the Sacramento delta would cost 2 percent of the value of the tomatoes on an acre.

[h]The cost of raising an offshore drilling platform 1 m is less than 1 percent of its total cost.

[i]Strengthening coastal properties for 100-mph wind would cost between a tenth and a third of current state and local service budgets for the entire United States. The cost of moving a house would be 1 to 4 times the present U.S. per capita GNP and a tenth to a half of that of 2100.

SOURCE: Chapter 3 of the Adaptation Panel report.

29. Are there possible consequences of greenhouse warming with highly adverse impacts?

Two have been identified.

• Deep ocean currents could be interrupted. Increased freshwater runoff in the Arctic might alter the salinity of northern oceans, thereby reducing or stopping the vertical flow of water into the deep ocean along Greenland and Iceland. This might interrupt a major deep ocean current running from the North Atlantic around the Cape of Good Hope and through the Indian Ocean to the Pacific. This could affect temperature and precipitation, with repercussions that might be catastrophic. Very little is currently known about the potential of this phenomenon.

• The West Antarctic Ice Sheet could surge. The Antarctic and Greenland ice sheets combined make up the world's largest reservoir of fresh water. The West Antarctic Ice Sheet alone contains enough water to raise global average sea level about 7 meters (23 feet). Warming could affect the speed at which the ice sheet flows to the sea and breaks off into icebergs. A large subsequent influx of fresh water could alter the salinity of the world's oceans, affecting currents and plant and animal populations alike. The ramifications are extreme, and it might lead to disruption of deep ocean currents and all that that entails. The timing of such a possibility is controversial. Current thinking is that it would take centuries, but there is little empirical evidence on which to base estimates.

30. What are appropriate responses to very uncertain, but highly adverse impacts?

Both individuals and societies must decide how to handle events that are very unlikely but which have severe consequences. Homeowners purchase insurance against the very unlikely event of fire. In essence, insurance is a cost today (the insurance premium) to avoid undesirable consequences later (losing one's possessions to fire). If we want to avoid unsure adverse impacts of possible climate change, we might want to spend money now that would reduce the likelihood that those things can happen. In principle, there are two different kinds of "climate insurance." We could do things that reduce the likelihood that the climate will change (mitigation options), or we could do things that reduce the sensitivity of affected human and natural systems to future climate change (adaptation options).

31. Does looking at potential impacts tell us where to set priorities for responding to greenhouse warming?

Partly. The examination of potential impacts can help provide rough estimates of the cost at which adaptation could be accomplished should climate change. This is an approximation of the "damage function" and can be used to assess how much to spend on emission reductions or offsets. However, all estimates are approximations with very little precision. The amount to allocate to prevent additional greenhouse warming depends significantly on the preferred degree of risk aversion.

PREVENTING OR REDUCING ADDITIONAL
GREENHOUSE WARMING

32.   What are the sources of greenhouse gas emissions?

All of the major greenhouse gases except CFCs are produced by both natural processes and human activity. Table A.4 summarizes the principal sources of greenhouse gases associated with human activity.

33.   What interventions could reduce greenhouse warming?

It is useful to examine two different aspects of reducing emissions or offsetting emissions:

• "Direct" reduction or offsetting of emissions through altering equipment, products, physical processes, or behaviors
• "Indirect" reduction or offsetting of emissions through altering the behavior of people in their economic or private lives and thus affecting the overall level of activity leading to emissions

It is much easier to estimate potential effectiveness and costs of direct reductions than of indirect incentives on human behavior. This is mostly because of the many factors that affect behavior in addition to the incentives in any particular program.

34.   How can specific mitigation options be compared?

Mitigation options can be compared quantitatively in terms of their cost-effectiveness and qualitatively in terms of the obstacles to their implementation and in terms of other benefits and costs.

The standard quantitative unit used to compare mitigation options is the cost per metric ton of carbon emissions reduced or per metric ton of carbon removed from the atmosphere. The amount of carbon can be converted to the amount of CO_2 in the atmosphere by multiplying by 3.67, which is the ratio of the molecular weights of carbon and CO_2. Other greenhouse gases can be "translated" to CO_2 equivalency by using two calculations. First, the amount of radiative forcing caused by a specific concentration of the gas is estimated in terms of the change in energy reaching the surface (in watts per square meter). This estimate accounts for atmospheric chemistry, atmospheric lifetime of the gas, and other relevant factors affecting the total contribution of that gas to greenhouse warming. Second, the amount of

TABLE A.4 Estimated 1985 Global Greenhouse Gas Emissions from Human Activities

	Greenhouse Gas Emissions (Mt/yr)	CO_2-equivalent Emissions[a] (Mt/yr)	
CO_2 Emissions			
Commercial energy	18,800	18,800	(57)
Tropical deforestation	2,600	2,600	(8)
Other	400	400	(1)
TOTAL	21,800	21,800	(66)
CH_4 Emissions			
Fuel production	60	1,300	(4)
Enteric fermentation	70	1,500	(5)
Rice cultivation	110	2,300	(7)
Landfills	30	600	(2)
Tropical deforestation	20	400	(1)
Other	30	600	(2)
TOTAL	320	6,700	(20)[b]
CFC-11 and CFC-12 Emissions			
TOTAL	0.6	3,200	(10)
N_2O Emissions			
Coal combustion	1	290	(>1)
Fertilizer use	1.5	440	(1)
Gain of cultivated land	0.4	120	(>1)
Tropical deforestation	0.5	150	(>1)
Fuel wood and industrial biomass	0.2	60	(>1)
Agricultural wastes	0.4	120	(>1)
TOTAL	4	1,180	(4)
TOTAL		32,880	(100)

[a]CO_2-equivalent emissions are calculated from the Greenhouse Gas Emissions column by using the following multipliers:

CO_2	1
CH_4	21
CFC-11 and -12	5,400
N_2O	290

Numbers in parentheses are percentages of total.

[b]Total does not sum due to rounding errors.

NOTE: Mt/yr = million (10^6) metric tons (t) per year. All entries are rounded because the exact values are controversial.

SOURCE: Adapted from U.S. Department of Energy. 1990. *The Economics of Long-Term Global Climate Change: A Preliminary Assessment—Report of an Interagency Task Force.* Springfield, Va.: National Technical Information Service.

CO_2 that would produce the same amount of forcing at the surface is calculated. This is the CO_2 equivalent for that specific concentration of the other greenhouse gas. The respective costs per ton for different options can then be compared directly. It is important to recognize, however, that these calculations allow comparison only of initial contributions. They do not account for changes in energy-trapping effectiveness over the various lifetimes of these gases in the atmosphere.

35. What mitigation options are most cost-effective?

The panel ranks options for reducing greenhouse gas emissions or removing greenhouse gases from the atmosphere according to their cost-effectiveness. Some of these options have net savings or very low net implementation costs compared to other investments. The options range from net savings to more than $100 per metric ton of CO_2-equivalent emissions avoided or removed from the atmosphere. The most cost-effective mitigation options are presented in Table A.5.

36. What are examples of options with large potential to reduce or offset emissions?

The so-called geoengineering options have the potential of substantially affecting atmospheric concentrations of greenhouse gases. They have the ability to screen incoming sunlight, stimulate uptake of CO_2 by plants and animals in the oceans, or remove CO_2 from the atmosphere. Although they appear feasible, they require additional investigation because of their potential environmental impacts.

37. How much would it cost to significantly reduce current U.S. greenhouse gas emissions?

It depends on the level of emission reduction desired and how it is done. The most cost-effective options are those that enhance efficient use of energy: efficiency improvements in lighting and appliances, white roofs and paving to enhance reflectivity, and improvement in building and construction practices.

Figure A.4 compares mitigation options, and Table A.5 gives the panel's estimates of net cost and emission reductions for several options. It must be emphasized that the table presents the panel's estimates of the *maximum* technical potential for each option. The calculation of cost-effectiveness of lighting efficiency, for example, does not consider whether the supply of light bulbs could meet the demand with current production capacities. Nor does it consider the trade-off between expenditures on light bulbs and on health care, education, or basic shelter for low-income families. In addition, there is a danger of some "double counting." For example, in the area of energy supply both nuclear and natural gas energy options assume re-

TABLE A.5 Comparison of Selected Mitigation Options in the United States

Mitigation Option	Net Implementation Cost[a]	Potential Emission[b] Reduction (t CO_2 equivalent per year)
Building energy efficiency	Net benefit	900 million[c]
Vehicle efficiency (no fleet change)	Net benefit	300 million
Industrial energy management	Net benefit to low cost	500 million
Transportation system management	Net benefit to low cost	50 million
Power plant heat rate improvements	Net benefit to low cost	50 million
Landfill gas collection	Low cost	200 million
Halocarbon-CFC usage reduction	Low cost	1400 million
Agriculture	Low cost	200 million
Reforestation	Low to moderate cost[d]	200 million
Electricity supply	Low to moderate cost[d]	1000 million[e]

[a]Net benefit = cost less than or equal to zero
Low cost = cost between $1 and $9 per ton of CO_2 equivalent
Moderate cost = cost between $10 and $99 per ton of CO_2 equivalent
High cost = cost of $100 or more per ton of CO_2 equivalent

[b]This "maximum feasible" potential emission reduction assumes 100 percent implementation of each option in reasonable applications and is an optimistic "upper bound" on emission reductions.

[c]This depends on the actual implementation level and is controversial. This represents a middle value of possible rates.

[d]Some portions do fall in low cost, but it is not possible to determine the amount of reductions obtainable at that cost.

[e]The potential emission reduction for electricity supply options is actually 1700 Mt CO_2 equivalent per year, but 1000 Mt is shown here to remove the double-counting effect.

NOTE: Here and throughout this report, tons are metric.

SOURCE: Chapter 11 of the Mitigation Panel report.

placement of the same coal-fired power plants. Table A.5, however, presents only options that avoid double counting. Finally, although there is evidence that efficiency programs can pay, there is no field evidence showing success with programs on the massive scale suggested here. Thus there may be very good reasons why "negative cost options" on the figure are not implemented today.

The United States could reduce its greenhouse gas emissions by between 10 and 40 percent of the 1990 levels at low cost, or perhaps some net savings, if proper policies are implemented.

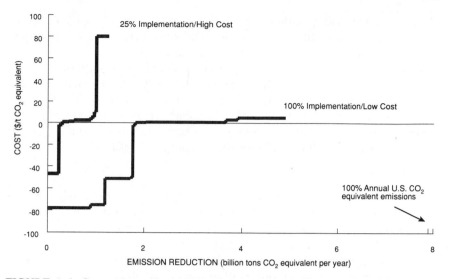

FIGURE A.4 Comparison of mitigation options. Total potential reduction of CO_2-equivalent emissions is compared to the cost in dollars per ton of CO_2 reduction. Options are ranked from left to right in CO_2 emissions according to cost. Some options show the possibility of reductions of CO_2 emissions at a net savings.

SOURCE: Chapter 11 of the report of the Mitigation Panel.

ADAPTING TO ADDITIONAL GREENHOUSE WARMING

38. Will human and natural systems adapt without assistance?

Farmers adjust their crops and cultivation practices in response to weather patterns over time. Natural ecosystems also adapt to changing conditions. The real issue is the rate at which human and natural systems will be able to adjust.

39. At what rates can human and natural systems adapt?

Many human systems have decision and investment cycles that are shorter than the time in which impacts of climate change would become manifest. These systems in the United States should be able to adjust to climate change without governmental intervention, as long as it is gradual and information about the rates of change is widely available. This applies to agriculture, commercial forestry, and most of industry. Industrial sectors with extremely long investment cycles (e.g., transport systems, urban infrastructure, and major structures and facilities) or requiring high volumes of water may require special attention. Coastal urban settlements would be able to react quickly (within 3 to 5 years) if sea level rises. Response would be much more difficult, however, where financial and other resources are limited, such as in many developing countries.

Some natural systems adjust at rates an order of magnitude or more slower than those anticipated for global-scale temperature changes. For example, the observed and theoretical migration of large trees with heavy seeds is an order of magnitude slower than the anticipated change in climate zones. Furthermore, natural ecosystems cannot anticipate climate change but must wait until after conditions have changed to respond.

40.   What is the value of the vulnerable natural ecosystems?

Natural ecosystems contribute commercial products, but their value is generally considered to exceed this contribution to the economy. For example, genetic resources are generally undervalued because people cannot capture the benefits of investments they might make in preserving biodiversity. Many species are unlikely to ever have commercial value, and it is virtually impossible to predict which ones will become marketable.

In addition, some people value natural systems regardless of their economic value. Loss of species, in their view, is undesirable whether or not those species have any commercial value. They generally hold that preservation of the potential for evolutionary change is a desirable goal in and of itself. Humanity, they claim, should not do things that alter the course of natural evolution. This view is sometimes also applied to humanity's cultural heritage—to buildings, music, art, and other cultural artifacts.

41.   How much would it cost to adapt to the anticipated climatic changes?

The panel's analysis suggests that some human and natural systems are not very sensitive to the anticipated climatic changes. These include most sectors of industry. Other systems are sensitive to climatic changes but can be adapted at a cost whose present value is small in comparison to the overall level of economic activity. These include agriculture, commercial forestry, urban coastal infrastructure, and tourism. Some systems are sensitive, and their adaptation is questionable. The unmanaged systems of plants and animals that occupy much of our lands and oceans adapt at a pace slower than the anticipated rate of climatic change. Their future under climate change would be problematic. Poor nations may also adapt painfully. Finally, some possible climatic changes like shifts in ocean currents have consequences that could be extremely severe, and thus the costs of adaptation might be very large. However, it is not currently possible to assess the likelihood of such cataclysmic changes.

No attempt has been made to comprehensively assess the costs of anticipated climatic changes on a global basis.

42. How much should be spent in response to greenhouse warming?

The answer depends on the estimated costs of prevention and the estimated damages from greenhouse warming. In addition, the likelihood and severity of extreme events, the discount rate, and the degree of risk aversion will modify this first-order approximation.

The appropriate level of expenditure depends on the value attached to the adverse outcomes compared to other allocations of available funds, human resources, and so on. In essence, the answer depends on the degree of risk aversion attached to adverse outcomes of climate change. The fact that less is known about the more adverse outcomes makes this a classic example of dealing with high-consequence, low-probability events. Programs that truly increase our knowledge and monitor relevant changes are especially needed.

IMPLEMENTING RESPONSE PROGRAMS

43. What policy instruments could be used to implement response options?

A wide array of policy instruments of two different types are available: regulation and incentives. Regulatory instruments mandate action, and include controls on consumption (bans, quotas, required product attributes), production (quotas on products or substances), factors in design or production (efficiency, durability, processes), and provision of services (mass transit, land use). Incentive instruments are designed to influence decisions by individuals and organizations and include taxes and subsidies on production factors (carbon tax, fuel tax), on products and other outputs (emission taxes, product taxes), financial inducements (tax credits, subsidies), and transferable emission rights (tradable emission reductions, tradable credits). The choice of policy instrument depends on the objective to be served.

44. At what level of society should actions be taken?

Interventions at all levels of human aggregation could effectively reduce greenhouse warming. For example, individuals could reduce energy consumption, recycle goods, and reduce consumption of deleterious materials. Local governments could control emissions from buildings, transport fleets, waste processing plants, and landfill dumps. State governments could restructure electric utility pricing structures and stimulate a variety of efficiency incentives. National governments could pursue action in most of the policy areas of relevance. International organizations could coordinate programs in various parts of the world, manage transfers of resources and technologies, and facilitate exchange of monitoring and other relevant data.

45. Is international action necessary?

The greenhouse phenomenon is global. Unilateral actions can contribute significantly, but national efforts alone would not be sufficient to eliminate the problem. The United States is the largest contributor of CO_2 emissions (with estimates ranging from 17 to 21 percent of the global total). But even if this country were to totally eliminate or offset its emissions, the effect on overall greenhouse warming might be lost if no other countries acted in concert with that aim.

46. What about differences between rich and poor countries?

Poor and developing countries are likely to be the most vulnerable to climate change. In addition, many developing countries today are sorely pressed in a variety of other ways. They may conclude that other issues have more immediate consequences for their citizens. Incentives in all parts of the world for intervention in the area of greenhouse warming may thus draw heavily on the industrialized nations. They may be called upon to help poor countries stimulate economic development and thus become better able to cope with climate change. They may also be asked to provide expertise and technologies to help poor countries adapt to the conditions they face.

ACTIONS TO BE TAKEN

47. Do scientific assessments of greenhouse warming tell us what to do?

Current scientific understanding of greenhouse warming is both incomplete and uncertain. Response depends in part on the degree of risk aversion attached to poorly understood, low-probability events with extremely adverse outcomes. Lack of scientific understanding should not be used as a justification for avoiding reasoned decisions about responses to possible additional greenhouse warming.

48. Is it better to prevent greenhouse warming now or wait and adapt to the consequences?

This complicated question has several parts.

• First, will it be possible to live with the consequences if nothing is done now? The panel's analysis suggests that advanced, industrialized countries will be able to adapt to most of the anticipated consequences of additional greenhouse warming without great economic hardship. In some regions, climate and related conditions may be noticeably worse, but in other regions better. Countries that currently face difficulty coping with extreme climatic events, or whose traditional coping mechanisms are breaking down, may be sorely pressed by the climatic changes accompanying an equivalent doubling of atmospheric CO_2 concentrations. It is important to recognize that there may be dramatic improvement or disastrous deterioration in specific locales. In addition, this analysis applies to the next 30 to 50 years. The situation may be different beyond that time horizon.

Natural communities of plants and animals, however, face much greater difficulties. Greenhouse warming would likely stress such ecosystems sufficiently to break them apart, resulting in a restructuring of the community in any given locale. New species would be likely to gain dominance, with a different overall mix of species. Some individual species would migrate to new, more livable locations. Greenhouse warming would most likely change the face of the natural landscape. Similar changes would occur in lakes and oceans.

In addition, there are possible extremely adverse consequences, such as changing ocean currents, that are poorly understood today. The response to such possibilities depends on the degree of risk aversion concerning those outcomes. The greater the degree of risk aversion, the greater the impetus for preventive action.

• Second, does it matter when interventions are made? Yes, for three different kinds of reasons. Because greenhouse gases have relatively long lifetimes in the atmosphere, and because of lags in the response of the system, their effect builds up over time. These time-dependent phenomena lead to the long-term "equilibrium" warming being greater than the "realized" warming at any given point in time. These dynamic aspects of the climate system show the importance of acting now to change traditional patterns of behavior that we have recently recognized to be detrimental, such as heavy reliance on fossil fuels. In addition, the implications of intervention programs for the overall economy vary with time. Gradual imposition of restraints is much less disruptive to the overall economy than their sudden application. Finally, the length of investment cycles can be crucial in determining the costs of intervention. In addition, some investments can be thought of as insurance, or payments now to avoid undesirable outcomes in the future. The choice is made more complicated by the fact that the outcomes are highly uncertain.

• Third, what discount rate should be used? The selection of a discount rate is very controversial. Macroeconomic calculations for the United States show a return on capital investment of 12 percent. The choice of discount rate reflects time preference. The panel has used discount rates of 3, 6, and 10 percent in its analysis. Finally, consumers often behave as if they have used a discount rate closer to 30 percent. The panel has also included this rate for comparison when options involve individual action.

49.   Are there special attributes of programs appropriate for response to greenhouse warming?

Yes. The uncertainties present in all aspects of climate change and our understanding of response to potential greenhouse warming place a high premium on information. Small-scale interventions that are both reversible and yield information about key aspects of the relevant phenomena are especially attractive for both mitigation and adaptation options. Monitoring of emission rates, climatic changes, and human and ecologic responses should yield considerable payoffs.

Perhaps the most important attribute of preferred policies is that they be able to accommodate surprises. They should be constructed so that they are flexible and can change if the nature or speed of stress is different than anticipated.

50.   What should be done now?

The panel developed a set of recommended options in five areas: reducing or offsetting emissions, enhancing adaptation to greenhouse warming, improving knowledge for future decisions, evaluating geoengineering options, and exercising international leadership.   The panel recommends moving decisively to undertake *all* of the actions described under questions 51 through 55 below.

51.   What can be done to reduce or offset emissions of greenhouse gases?

Three areas dominate the panel's analysis of reducing or offsetting current emissions: eliminating CFC emissions and developing substitutes that minimize or eliminate greenhouse gas emissions, changing energy policy, and utilizing forest offsets. Eliminating CFC emissions has the biggest single contribution. Recommendations concerning energy policy are to examine how to make the price of energy reflect all health, environmental, and other social costs with a goal of gradual introduction of such a system; to make conservation and efficiency the chief element in energy policy; and to consider the full range of supply, conversion, end use, and external effects in planning future energy supply. Global deforestation should be reduced, and a moderate domestic reforestation program should be explored.

52.   What can be done now to help people and natural systems of plants and animals adapt to future greenhouse warming?

Most of the actions that can be taken today improve the capability of the affected systems to deal with current climatic variability. Options include maintaining agricultural basic, applied, and experimental research; making water supplies more robust by coping with present variability; taking into consideration possible climate change in the margins of safety for long-lived structures; and reducing present rates of loss in biodiversity.

53. What can be done to improve knowledge for future decisions?

Action is needed in several areas. Collection and dissemination of data that provide an uninterrupted record of the evolving climate and of data that are needed for the improvement and testing of climate models should be expanded. Weather forecasts should be improved, especially of extremes, for weeks and seasons to ease adaptation to climate change. The mechanisms that play a significant role in the responses of the climate to changing concentrations of greenhouse gases need further identification, and quantification at scales appropriate for climate models. Field research should be conducted on entire systems of species over many years to learn how CO_2 enrichment and other facets of greenhouse warming alter the mix of species and changes in total production or quality of biomass. Research on social and economic aspects of global change and greenhouse warming should be strengthened.

54. Do geoengineering options really have potential?

Preliminary assessments of these options suggest that they have large potential to mitigate greenhouse warming and are relatively cost-effective in comparison to other mitigation options. However, their feasibility and especially the side-effects associated with them need to be carefully examined. Because the geoengineering options have the potential to affect greenhouse warming on a substantial scale, because there is convincing evidence that some of these cause or alter a variety of chemical reactions in the atmosphere, and because the climate system is poorly understood, such options must be considered extremely carefully. If greenhouse warming occurs, and the climate system turns out to be highly sensitive to radiative forcing, they may be needed.

55. What should the United States do at the international level?

The United States should resume full participation in international programs to slow population growth and contribute its share to their financial and other support. In addition, the United States should participate fully in international agreements and programs to address greenhouse warming, including representation by officials at an appropriate level.

Appendix B
Background Information on Synthesis Panel Members and Professional Staff

SYNTHESIS PANEL MEMBERS

The Honorable DANIEL J. EVANS, Chairman, is chairman of Daniel J. Evans & Associates in Seattle, Washington. A registered civil and structural engineer, he served as U.S. Senator from the State of Washington from 1983 to 1989, and as governor from 1965 to 1977. He was president of The Evergreen State College from 1977 to 1983 and chaired the Pacific Northwest Power and Conservation Planning Council from 1981 to 1983. He is a member of the National Academy of Public Administration.

ROBERT McCORMICK ADAMS is secretary of the Smithsonian Institution in Washington, D.C. An anthropologist and educator, he conducted field research on the history of irrigation and urban settlements. Formerly provost at the University of Chicago, he is a member of the National Academy of Sciences.

GEORGE F. CARRIER is T. Jefferson Coolidge Professor of Applied Mathematics, emeritus, at Harvard University in Cambridge, Massachusetts. He specializes in mathematical modeling of fluid dynamics. He chaired the 1985 National Research Council Committee on Atmospheric Effects of Nuclear Explosions. He is a member of the National Academy of Sciences and the National Academy of Engineering.

RICHARD N. COOPER is professor of economics at Harvard University in Cambridge, Massachusetts, and a director of the Federal Reserve Bank of Boston. He served as a member of the Council of Economic Advisors from 1961 to 1963. From 1972 to 1974 he was provost at Yale University. He was Undersecretary of State for Economic Affairs from 1977 to 1981.

ROBERT A. FROSCH is vice president at General Motors Research Laboratories in Warren, Michigan. He was Assistant Secretary of the Navy for Research and Development from 1966 to 1973. From 1973 to 1975 he was assistant executive director of the United Nations Environment Program. He was director of the National Aeronautics and Space Administration from 1977 to 1981. He is a member of the National Academy of Engineering.

THOMAS H. LEE is professor emeritus in the Department of Electrical Engineering and Computer Science at the Massachusetts Institute of Technology in Cambridge. He worked at General Electric for 32 years and from 1978 to 1980 was staff executive and chief technologist. From 1980 to 1984 he directed the Electric Power Systems Engineering Laboratory at the Massachusetts Institute of Technology, and was director of the International Institute for Applied Systems Analysis from 1984 to 1987. He is a member of the National Academy of Engineering.

JESSICA TUCHMAN MATHEWS is vice president at the World Resources Institute in Washington, D.C. A molecular biologist and policy analyst, she was professional staff to the U.S. Congress House Interior Committee from 1974 to 1975. From 1977 to 1979, she was director of the Office for Global Issues at the National Security Council.

WILLIAM D. NORDHAUS is professor of economics at Yale University in New Haven, Connecticut. He was a member of the Council of Economic Advisors from 1977 to 1979. From 1986 to 1988 he was provost at Yale University.

GORDON H. ORIANS is professor of zoology and was formerly director of the Institute for Environmental Studies at the University of Washington in Seattle. He specializes in evolution of vertebrate species. He is a member of the National Academy of Sciences.

STEPHEN H. SCHNEIDER is head of Interdisciplinary Climate Systems at the National Center for Atmospheric Research in Boulder, Colorado. He is an expert on global climate change models and is editor of *Climate Change.*

MAURICE F. STRONG served on the panel until February 1990, when he resigned due to his commitment to serve as secretary general to the 1992 United Nations Conference on Environment and Development. He was director general of the External Aid Office of the Canadian government and undersecretary general of the United Nations with responsibility for environmental affairs. He was chief executive of the 1972 United Nations Conference on the Human Environment.

SIR CRISPIN TICKELL is warden of Green College, Oxford, United Kingdom. He entered the British diplomatic service in 1954. From 1984 to 1987 he was permanent secretary of the Overseas Development Administration in the United Kingdom. From 1987 to 1990 he was permanent representative of the United Kingdom to the United Nations. He is author of *Climate Change and World Affairs.*

VICTORIA J. TSCHINKEL is senior consultant with Landers and Parsons in Tallahassee, Florida. From 1981 to 1987 she was secretary of the Florida Department of Environmental Regulation. An expert on environmental regulation and management, she is a member of the National Academy of Public Administration. She is also a member of the Electric Power Research Institute Advisory Council and the Advisory Committee for Nuclear Facility Safety.

PAUL E. WAGGONER is distinguished scientist at the Connecticut Agricultural Experiment Station in New Haven. He chaired the American Association for the Advancement of Science Panel on Climatic Variability, Climate Change, and the Planning and Management of United States Water Resources. He is a member of the National Academy of Sciences.

PROFESSIONAL STAFF

ROB COPPOCK is staff director for the Panel on Policy Implications of Greenhouse Warming of the Committee on Science, Engineering, and Public Policy of the National Academy of Sciences, the National Academy of Engineering, and the Institute of Medicine in Washington, D.C. From 1976 to 1984 he was staff scientist at the International Institute for Environment and Society in Berlin, Germany. He has been on the staff at the National Academy of Sciences since 1985. He currently is chairman of the Global Risk Analysis Division of the Society for Risk Analysis.

NANCY A. CROWELL is administrative specialist for the Panel on Policy Implications of Greenhouse Warming of the Committee on Science, Engineering, and Public Policy of the National Academy of Sciences, the National Academy of Engineering, and the Institute of Medicine in Washington, D.C.

DEBORAH D. STINE is staff officer for the Panel on Policy Implications of Greenhouse Warming of the Committee on Science, Engineering, and Public Policy of the National Academy of Sciences, the National Academy of Engineering, and the Institute of Medicine in Washington, D.C. Her specialties are environmental engineering and policy analysis. From 1983 to 1988 she was an air pollution engineer with the Texas Air Pollution Control Board. From 1988 to 1989 she was an air issues manager at the Chemical Manufacturers Association.

Appendix C
Membership Lists for
Effects, Mitigation, and
Adaptation Panels

EFFECTS PANEL

GEORGE F. CARRIER (Chairman), Division of Applied Science, Harvard University, Cambridge, Massachusetts

WILFRIED BRUTSAERT, School of Civil and Environmental Engineering, Cornell University, Ithaca, New York

ROBERT D. CESS, Institute for Terrestrial and Planetary Atmospheres, State University of New York, Stony Brook

HERMAN CHERNOFF, Department of Statistics, Harvard University, Cambridge, Massachusetts

ROBERT E. DICKINSON, National Center for Atmospheric Research, Boulder, Colorado

JOHN IMBRIE, Department of Geological Sciences, Brown University, Providence, Rhode Island

THOMAS B. KARL, National Climate Data Center, Asheville, North Carolina

MICHAEL C. MacCRACKEN, Atmospheric and Geophysical Sciences Division, Lawrence Livermore Laboratory, Livermore, California

BERRIEN MOORE, Institute for the Study of Earth, Oceans, and Space, University of New Hampshire, Durham

MITIGATION PANEL

THOMAS H. LEE (Chairman), Department of Electrical Engineering and Computer Science, Massachusetts Institute of Technology, Cambridge

PETER BREWER, Monterey Bay Aquarium Research Institute, Pacific Grove, California

EDITH BROWN-WEISS, Georgetown University, Washington, D.C.
(resigned from panel May 17, 1990)

RICHARD N. COOPER, Harvard University, Cambridge, Massachusetts

ROBERT CRANDALL, Brookings Institute, Washington, D.C.

ROBERT EVENSON, Economic Growth Center, Yale University, New
Haven, Connecticut

DOUGLAS FOY, Conservation Law Foundation, Boston, Massachusetts

ROBERT A. FROSCH, General Motors Research Laboratories, Warren,
Michigan

RICHARD GARWIN, Thomas J. Watson Research Center, Yorktown
Heights, New York

JOSEPH GLAS, Freon Products Division, E.I. du Pont de Nemours,
Wilmington, Delaware

KAI N. LEE, Department of Political Science and Institute for
Environmental Studies, University of Washington, Seattle, and Institute
of Economic Research, Kyoto University, Japan

GREGG MARLAND, Environmental Science Division, Oak Ridge
National Laboratory, Oak Ridge, Tennessee

JESSICA TUCHMAN MATHEWS, World Resources Institute,
Washington, D.C.

ARTHUR H. ROSENFELD, University of California, Berkeley, and
Center for Building Science, Lawrence Berkeley Laboratory, Berkeley,
California

EDWARD S. RUBIN, Mechanical Engineering and Public Policy, and
Center for Energy and Environmental Studies, Carnegie Mellon
University, Pittsburgh, Pennsylvania

MILTON RUSSELL, Economic, Energy, Environment and Resources
Center, University of Tennessee, Knoxville, and Oak Ridge National
Laboratory, Oak Ridge, Tennessee

STEPHEN H. SCHNEIDER, Interdisciplinary Climate Systems, National
Center for Atmospheric Research, Boulder, Colorado

EUGENE B. SKOLNIKOFF, Massachusetts Institute of Technology,
Cambridge

THOMAS H. STIX, Plasma Physics Laboratory, Princeton University,
Princeton, New Jersey

ADAPTATION PANEL

PAUL E. WAGGONER (Chairman), Connecticut Agricultural Experiment
Station, New Haven

JESSE AUSUBEL, Rockefeller University, New York, New York

CLARK BINKLEY, Faculty of Forestry, University of British Columbia,
Vancouver, British Columbia, Canada

MARY M. KRITZ, Population and Development Program, Cornell University, Ithaca, New York

JOSHUA LEDERBERG, Rockefeller University, New York, New York

WILLIAM LEWIS, McKinsey and Company, Washington, D.C.

JON C. LIEBMAN, Civil Engineering Department, University of Illinois, Urbana

JANE LUBCHENCO, Department of Zoology, Oregon State University, Corvallis

WILLIAM D. NORDHAUS, Department of Economics, Yale University, New Haven, Connecticut

GORDON H. ORIANS, Department of Zoology and Institute for Environmental Studies, University of Washington, Seattle

WILLIAM E. RIEBSAME, Natural Hazards Research and Applications Information Center, University of Colorado, Boulder

NORMAN J. ROSENBERG, Climate Resources Program, Resources for the Future, Washington, D.C.

DANIEL P. SHEER, Water Resources Management, Columbia, Maryland

SIR CRISPIN TICKELL, Green College, Oxford, England

Index

A

Absorption rates, of greenhouse gases, 10, 11
Ad Hoc Working Group of Government Representatives to Prepare for Negotiations on a Framework Convention on Climate Change , 66
Adaptation
    actions to assist human and natural systems in, 112
    and climate change, 28, 32–33, 42–45, 108
    costs of, 99–101
    evaluation of options in, 41–42
    impacts and capacities of, 36–40, 100–101, 107–108
    indices used in, 40–41
    methods of, 34–35
    mitigation vs., 28
    panel recommendations for enhancing, 76–78
    as policy option, 30, 32–33
    role of innovation in, 35–36
Agriculture
    adaptability of, 42–44
    effect of changes in precipitation and evaporation on, 37
    effect of increased atmospheric concentration of carbon dioxide on, 36–37, 77
    impact on national economy, 42–43
    nonenergy emission reduction for, 57

    panel recommendations regarding, 76–77
Alternative fuels, 55
Animal life, responses to climate changes by, 35, 37–38
Annualized costs, determining, 31
Annualized emission reductions, 31
Atmospheric lifetime of greenhouse gases, 11, 88, 89, 103
Atmospheric transformation rate
    extrapolation of current, 11, 13
    of greenhouse gases, 10–12

B

Backstop technology, 50, 51
Biodiversity. See also Ecosystems
    impact of climate change on, 33, 35–38
    panel recommendations regarding, 77–80
Blooms, indices to monitor variations in, 41
Board on Atmospheric Sciences and Climate (National Research Council), 18
Bridges, 41, 77
Building codes, 39

C

Carbon cycle, 88
Carbon dioxide (CO_2)
    atmospheric concentrations of, 2, 10–12, 25, 85, 87
    effects of increased concentration of, 36–37, 79–80

equivalency calculations, 31, 103
  as greenhouse gas, 1, 85
  movement among sinks of, 88
  and temperature in prehistoric past, 87–
    88
Carbon dioxide (CO_2) emissions
  annualized costs and annualized
    reduction of, 31
  dispersion of, 10
  equivalent doubling of preindustrial
    level of, 25, 94–95
  estimates of, 5–8
  impact of deforestation on, 9, 75, 76
  per unit of economic activity, 8–9
  radiative forcing and, 13, 103, 105
CFC-12, 88–89. *See also*
    Chlorofluorocarbons
CFC-115, 88. *See also* Chlorofluorocarbons
CFCs. *See* Chlorofluorocarbons
CH_4 (Methane). *See* Methane (CH_4);
    Methane (CH_4) emissions
Chlorofluorocarbon (CFC) emissions
  atmospheric concentrations of, 11, 25,
    85, 87
  estimates of, 5, 6
  lasers to remove atmospheric, 58
  panel recommendations regarding, 73,
    112
  regulatory interventions to control, 69,
    112
  results of eliminating, 52
Chlorofluorocarbons (CFCs)
  atmospheric lifetime of CFC-115, 88
  as greenhouse gas, 1, 85
  varying properties of, 11, 88–89
Clean Air Act, 52, 69
Climate
  elements that affect, 20, 23, 88
  understanding of, 24
Climate change
  adaptation to, 28, 32–33, 42–45, 108.
    See also Adaptation
  cataclysmic, 44–45
  facets of, 3
  general circulation models to predict,
    17–19, 92–93. *See also* General
    circulation models
  human responses to, 34, 36, 98, 99,
    107
  impact of projected, 97–101
  international agreement on, 66, 82
  research needs on, 69–70

Climate change sensitivities
  of agriculture, 37, 43
  of carbon dioxide fertilization of green
    plants, 36–37, 43
  of human health, 39–40, 43
  of industry and energy, 39, 43
  of managed forests and grasslands, 37,
    43
  of marine and coastal environments, 38,
    43
  of migration, 40, 43
  of natural landscape, 37–38, 43
  of political tranquility, 40, 43
  of settlements and coastal structures, 39,
    43
  of tourism and recreation, 39, 43
  of water resources, 38–39, 43
Climate models
  information to be gained through use of,
    17–19, 25
  panel recommendations regarding
    improvement and testing of, 78–79
Cloud stimulation, 58, 60, 81
CO_2. *See* Carbon dioxide (CO_2)
Coastal environments, adaptive capacity of,
    38
Commercial energy management, 54–55
Coral reefs, 44
Cost-benefit balancing, 52, 63, 96
Cost-effectiveness
  of mitigation options, 47, 49, 53, 59, 60,
    96, 105, 106
  of mitigation policy planning, 49–51
  role of, 48
  social goals and, 52
Costing, technological, 48–49
Costs
  annualized, 31
  for impacts of projected climate change,
    98–101
  negative, 50, 106
  to reduce current U.S. greenhouse gas
    emissions, 63, 105–107, 109

D

Data collection
  climate models used for, 17–19
  panel recommendations regarding, 70,
    78–80
  of sea level, 23–24
  of temperature records, 20–23

Deforestation. *See also* Forests
  issues raised by, 65
  panel recommendations regarding, 75–76
  in tropics, 9, 75–76
Developing countries
  agreements for phaseout of halocarbon emissions in, 73
  greenhouse gas emissions in, 4, 7–9, 64
  low-cost mitigation options in, 47
  participation in reduction programs by, 64
  special problems of, 110
  tropical deforestation in, 76
  varying capacities of, 41, 68
Discount rates
  determining appropriate, 29–30, 111
  mitigation options and, 53
  used to assign values to future outcomes, 28
Double-counting, 59, 61, 106

E

Earth, radiation balance of, 12, 14–17
Earth Observing System (EOS), 78
Economic issues, research dealing with, 70, 80
Economic well-being
  mitigation vs. adaptation and, 28, 29
  relationship between greenhouse gas emissions and, 4
Ecosystems. *See also* Biodiversity
  adaptive capacity of, 37–38, 43, 44
  responses to climatic changes by, 35
  value of natural, 33, 108
Eemian interglacial period, 87
Efficiency enhancement
  and "best practice," 28
  mitigation options involving, 54–59
  panel recommendations regarding, 73–74
Electricity
  efficiency measures for, 54–55
  mitigation options of, 56–57
Energy
  sensitivity to climate change, 39, 43
  social cost pricing of, 73
Energy conservation
  mitigation options involving, 54–59
  panel recommendations regarding, 73–74

Energy management mitigation options
  industrial, 55
  residential and commercial, 54–55
  transportation, 55–56
Energy modeling
  mitigation options using, 62
  technological costing vs., 48–49
Energy policy panel recommendations, 72–75
Energy supply mix, 74–75
Equilibrium temperature
  explanation of, 17, 93
  increases, 18
  possible impacts on, 16
Evaporation
  affecting water supply, 38
  effect of changes on agriculture, 37, 42–43

F

Farming. *See* Agriculture
Feedback mechanism, 92, 95
Financial resources, 33, 42. *See also* Developing countries
Forests
  management of, 37
  panel recommendations regarding, 72, 73, 75–76
  sensitivity assessment of, 36, 37, 43
  tropical, 9, 75–76
Fossil fuels
  consumption by developing countries of, 64
  effects of burning, 4, 27, 30–31
  replacement options for, 56–57, 75
France, greenhouse gas emissions in, 8, 9
Free-standing actions, 28
Full social cost pricing
  considerations regarding, 67, 68
  explanation of, 30–31
  panel recommendations regarding, 73

G

GCMs. *See* General circulation models
General circulation models (GCMs)
  to anticipate climatic changes, 17–18
  explanation of, 1–2, 92–93
  limitations to use of, 18–19, 94
  varying interpretations of, 18
Genetic resources, 33

Geoengineering
    assessment of options in, 113
    mitigation options, 53, 57–60, 105
    panel recommendations for evaluating
        options of, 70, 80–81
Global average temperature
    adaptation resulting from predicted rise
        in, 45–46
    effect of greenhouse gases on, 20, 22,
        25, 26, 85
    equilibrium, 16–18, 93
    as indicator of climatic effects, 3, 19
    recent changes in, 20, 87
    use of general circulation models to
        predict, 18
Government intervention, 63, 69, 109
Grasslands
    adaptive capacity of, 37
    sensitivity and adaptability of, 43
Greenhouse effect
    explanation of, 85–87
    knowledge and predictions regarding,
        85–95
Greenhouse gas emissions
    cost for achieving reductions in, 49–51,
        105–107
    human activities affecting, 3–4, 5–11,
        25, 88, 103, 104
    impact of economic and population
        growth on, 4–5. *See also* Population
        growth
    influence of climate on, 1, 79
    international considerations regarding
        control of, 64–66
    mitigation options for elimination of,
        54–58
    panel recommendations for reducing or
        offsetting, 70, 72–76, 112
    social and economic processes
        generating, 6, 70, 104
Greenhouse gases
    activities causing release of, 3–4
    atmospheric lifetime of, 11, 88, 89, 103
    atmospheric transformation rate in,
        10–12, 13
    characteristics of, 88–89. *See also*
        individual gases
    impacts on global equilibrium temperature
        of changes in atmospheric concentrations
        of, 16, 17
    list of, 1
    various properties of, 10–11

Greenhouse warming
    actions to be taken regarding, 110–113
    adapting to additional, 107–109. *See
        also* Adaptation
    costs and benefits attributable to, 52
    estimating future, 16, 17–19, 24–26, 93
    events possible due to, 1–2, 25–26
    explanation of, 1, 3, 85, 87
    framework for responding to, 70, 96
    impact of additional, 97–103
    implementing response options to, 109–110
    known facts regarding, 24–25, 27, 93–94
    limitations of human responses to, 41–42
    panel recommendations. *See* Panel
        recommendations
    policy options to deal with. *See* Policy
        options
    preventing or reducing additional, 95,
        103–107, 109
    sea level change due to, 23–24
    social and economic aspects of, 70, 80
    strategic indices of, 40–41

H

Halocarbons. *See also* Chlorofluorocarbons
    mitigation options for, 57
    panel recommendations for eliminating,
        72, 73
Hardware, technological, 35
HCFCs (Hydrogenated chlorofluorocarbons),
    1, 85
Health, human, 39–40, 42, 43
Holocene optimum, 87
Human activities affecting greenhouse gas
    emissions, 3–4, 5–11, 25, 88, 103, 104
Human adaptation
    to climate change, 34, 36, 98, 99, 107
    role of innovation in, 35–36, 96
Human health, 39–40, 42, 43
Human migration
    indices to monitor variations in, 41
    as response to climate change, 40, 43
Human settlements, sensitivity to climate
    change, 39, 43
Hydrogenated chlorofluorocarbons
    (HCFCs), 1, 85

I

Incentive policy instruments, 62, 63, 69, 109
India, greenhouse gas emissions in, 7

Indices, for monitoring purposes, 40–41
Industrial energy management, 55, 74
Industrialized countries
    agreements for phaseout of halocarbon
        emissions in, 73
    varying capacities of, 68
Industry, sensitivity to climate change, 39,
        42, 43
Information, as limiting factor in
        responding to greenhouse warming,
        42
Innovation, 35–36
Intergovernmental Panel on Climate Change
        (IPCC), 18, 65, 67
International cooperation
    importance of, 64, 110, 113
    panel recommendations for exercising
        leadership in, 70, 81–82
    for population control, 81
International Council of Scientific Unions
        (ICSU), 65
International Geosphere-Biosphere Program
        (IGBP), 65
International organizations
    activities of, 65–66, 109
    program coordination by, 63

L

Land air temperature measurement, 21
Land use planning, 39
Landfills, reduction of gas generation in, 57
Law of the Sea, 66
Levees, 77
Living standards, environmental
        degradation accompanying, 4
Local government, actions to control
        greenhouse warming by, 63
London Protocol, 66, 73

M

Margin of safety planning, 77
Marine ecosystems, 38, 43, 44
Mathews, Jessica, 45n–46n
Melting, high-latitude tundra, 24
Methane (CH_4)
    atmospheric lifetime of, 88
    as greenhouse gas, 1, 85
Methane (CH_4) emissions
    atmospheric concentrations of, 10, 11,
        25, 85, 87

due to melting of high-latitude tundra, 24
    estimates for 1985, 5, 6
Migration. *See* Human migration
Mitigation
    adaptation vs., 28, 29
    analysis of costs of, 47
    as policy option, 30–32, 67
Mitigation options
    assessment of, 51–60, 63
    comparison of, 49–51, 59–62, 103, 105–
        107
    cost-effectiveness of, 47, 49, 53, 59, 60,
        96, 105, 106
    for developing countries, 4, 47
    for electricity and fuel supply, 56–57
    geoengineering, 53, 57–60, 105
    implementation of, 62–63
    for industrial energy management, 55
    for nonenergy emission reduction, 57
    for residential and commercial energy
        management, 54–55
    technological costing vs. energy
        modeling for, 48–49
    for transportation energy management,
        55–56
Montreal Protocol on Protection of the
        Ozone Layer, 66, 73

N

National governments
    actions to control greenhouse warming
        by, 63, 109
    U.S. research budget, 69
Natural landscapes
    adaptive capacity of, 37
    sensitivity to change, 43
Negative feedback, 92, 95
Nitrous oxide (N_2O), 1, 85
Nitrous oxide (N_2O) emissions, 5, 6
N_2O (Nitrous oxide), 1, 85. *See also*
        Nitrous oxide (N_2O) emissions
Noneconomic values, 33
Nonenergy emission reduction, 57
Nuclear power
    concerns regarding, 53
    reactor design needs for, 75

O

O_3 (Ozone), 1, 85
Ocean biomass stimulation, 58, 60, 81

Ocean currents
    indices to monitor variability of, 40
    interruption of, 24, 102
Oceans
    research needs regarding, 79, 111
    sensitivity assessment of, 38
    surface temperature of, 21, 95
    thermal expansion in, 23–24
Ozone (O$_3$), 1, 85

P

Panel recommendations
    enhancing adaptation to greenhouse
        warming, 70, 76–78, 112
    evaluating geoengineering options, 70,
        80–81, 112
    exercising international leadership, 70,
        81–82, 112
    improving knowledge for future
        decisions, 70, 78–80, 112
    reducing or offsetting greenhouse gas
        emissions, 70, 72–76, 112
Parameterizations, 18
People's Republic of China, greenhouse gas
    emissions in, 7
Photosynthesis, effect of increased
        atmospheric concentration of carbon
        dioxide on, 37
Plant life, responses to climatic changes by,
    35, 37–38
Pliocene climate optimum, 87, 88
Policy considerations
    capacities of industrialized and
        developing countries as, 41, 68
    fundamental and applied research as,
        69–70
    taxes and incentives as, 69
Policy options
    assigning values to future outcomes and,
        29–30
    limited resources and, 33
    method of comparing, 30–33
    panel recommendations regarding,
        70–82. See also Panel
        recommendations
    risk perception and, 33
    types of, 27–28
Politics, sensitivity to climate change, 40,
    43
Pollution, increased living standards
        resulting in, 4

Population growth
    in developing countries, 64
    global, 5, 64, 81
    relationship between greenhouse gas
        emissions and, 4, 64, 81
Positive feedback, 92, 95
Precipitation
    agricultural changes due to changes in,
        37
    effect of climate changes on, 38–39, 42–
        43
    efficiency management to cope with
        variability in, 77

R

Radiation balance, 12, 14–17, 85, 86
Radiative energy emissions, 14
Radiative forcing
    caused by concentrations of carbon
        dioxide, 13, 103, 105
    explanation of, 11, 87
    geoengineering options affecting, 80
    of greenhouse gases from 1990 to 2030,
        13, 16, 17, 89–92
    research needs to understand phenomena
        affecting, 70
    role of chlorofluorocarbons in, 73
Real income, mitigation vs. adaptation and,
    28, 29
Recreation, sensitivity to climate change,
    39, 43, 44
Reforestation. See also Forests
    as mitigation option, 57
    panel recommendations regarding, 76
Regulatory policy instruments, 62–63, 109
Relative sea level (RSL), 23
Research
    international activities in, 65–66
    need for fundamental and applied, 69–
        70
    panel recommendations regarding, 70,
        78–80, 82
Residential energy management, 54–55
Resources, varying constraint felt by limited
        natural and human, 33
Risk perception, 33

S

Sea level
    effect on wetlands of, 38

global warming producing rise in, 26, 38
indices to monitor variations in, 41
variations in, 23–24
Sea surface temperatures, 21, 95
Second World Climate Conference, 65–67
Sensitivity
classifications of, 42–45, 97–99
definition of, 43, 99
development of economical adaptation
that lessens, 41
estimation of, 97
to natural phenomena, 36
Sensitivity assessment
of agriculture, 37
of carbon dioxide fertilization of green
plants, 36–37
data and analyses used, 36, 76
of human health, 39–40
of industry and energy, 39
of managed forests and grasslands, 37
of marine and coastal environment, 38
of natural landscape, 37–38
of political tranquility, 40
of settlements and coastal structures, 39
of tourism and recreation, 39
of water resources, 38–39
Sinks, 88
Social issues
greenhouse gas emission reduction
options and, 52
research dealing with, 70, 80
Software, technological, 35
Solar radiation, 12, 14, 15
State government, actions to control
greenhouse warming by, 63
Stratospheric particle options, 58, 60, 81
Sulfate aerosol emissions, 20
Sunlight screening, as mitigation option, 58

T

Taxes, as policy option, 69, 109
Technological costing
energy modeling vs., 48–49
mitigation options using, 62
Technological hardware and software, 35
Temperature records
interpretation of, 20–23
and occurrence of greenhouse warming,
92
and use of general circulation models,
18–19

Temperature variations
prehistoric, 23, 87–88
sulfate aerosol emissions as reason for,
20
Thermal expansion, of oceans, 23–24
Tide gauges, 23
Time, as limiting factor in responding to
greenhouse warming, 41
Tourism, 39, 43, 44
Transpiration, 36, 37
Transportation energy management, 55–56,
74
Tropics, deforestation in, 9, 75–76
Tundra melting, 24

U

United Nations Environment Programme,
65
United Nations World Conference on
Environment and Development
(1992), 66, 82
Urban settlements, 39, 43

V

Vehicle efficiency, 55

W

Water, as limiting factor in responding to
greenhouse warming, 41–42
Water resources
effect of climate changes on, 38
indices monitoring variations in streams
and soils, 40
management of, 38–39
panel recommendations regarding, 77
sensitivity and adaptability of, 43
Water vapor
and example of feedback mechanism, 92
as greenhouse gas, 1, 85
Weather. *See also* Climate change
impact of extreme, 34, 95
improvement in forecasting, 79
West Antarctic Ice Sheet, 23, 24, 102
Wetlands, 38
Wind patterns, 38
World Climate Program (WCP), 65
World Climate Research Program (WCRP),
65
World Meteorological Organization, 65

4398